ACHIEVE THE IMPOSSIBLE

How to Overcome Challenges and
Gain Success in Life, Work an

Professor Greg Whyte OB

BANTAM PRESS

LONDON · TORONTO · SYDNEY · AUCKLAND · JOHANNESBURG

TRANSWORLD PUBLISHERS
61–63 Uxbridge Road, London W5 5SA
www.transworldbooks.co.uk

Transworld is part of the Penguin Random House group of companies
whose addresses can be found at global.penguinrandomhouse.com

First published in Great Britain in 2015 by Bantam Press
an imprint of Transworld Publishers

A CIP catalogue record for this book
is available from the British Library.

ISBN 9780593075166

Typeset in 11/14pt Electra by Falcon Oast Graphic Art Ltd.
Printed and bound by Clays Ltd, Bungay, Suffolk.

Penguin Random House is committed to a sustainable
future for our business, our readers and our planet. This book
is made from Forest Stewardship Council® certified paper.

MIX
Paper from
responsible sources
FSC
www.fsc.org   FSC® C016897

1 3 5 7 9 10 8 6 4 2

CONTENTS

To Penny

FOREWORD

by David Walliams, Davina McCall and John Bishop

David Walliams:

Whatever you do, please, I beg you, do not read this book. Take it back to the shop and demand a refund. Burn it. Bury it. Perhaps it's best to burn it and then bury it just to be sure.

A decade ago I was a chubby camp comedian, best known for wearing a dress on television and saying 'I'm a lady' over and over again. Then I met Professor Greg Whyte. For some bizarre reason he thought he could train me to swim the English Channel. 'It's only twenty-two miles, and it should take eleven or twelve hours,' he said.

'How warm is the water?' I asked.

'Like a hot bath!' he replied with a smile. 'Fifteen degrees.'

As the BBC cameras were rolling and it was for charity, I realized it was impossible to pull out. In the autumn of 2005 Professor Greg Whyte began training me. I was someone who had failed their Cub Scout sports badge, something it is all but impossible to do. But by the summer of 2006 I had swum the Channel in record time and raised a million pounds, half of which I gave to charity.

As I was wiping off the grease at Dover harbour I thought, 'Thank the Lord I'll never have to do anything like that again!'

But no.

Oh no.

Professor Greg Whyte had other plans. Next I was to swim the Straits of Gibraltar from Europe to Africa in shark-infested waters. Then I was to cycle from John O'Groats to Land's End. After that I thought I had really earned the right to sit on my arse and watch *Strictly* and eat cake for the rest of my life. Just to be safe I changed my phone number, moved house and the police even gave me a new identity.

Somehow he found me.

The Professor had a new plan. I was to swim the length of the River Thames. 140 miles in just eight days. Bastard.

Professor Greg Whyte is the country's leading expert in sports science and is the man behind every single Sport Relief challenge. He has never accepted a penny for giving up weeks, months, even years of his time, and with myself, John Bishop, Davina McCall and others he has raised millions and millions of pounds for charity.

If he can inspire me to achieve the impossible, he can inspire you too.

David Walliams

Davina McCall:

When I was asked to do my 500 mile endurance challenge I said, 'Yes!!!'

Then I started thinking about it. I had an injury and was struggling to walk upstairs. I work; I've got three kids. I started crying every day. That is not an exaggeration. I honestly thought I could possibly die. How on earth could little old me do something like that?

Then I saw Greg. I cried at that meeting … and cried at almost every training session with him afterwards. It was my release – of fear, of tension. He told me that these feelings would be replaced with confidence, and I just had to trust him.

Looking back, he had me achieve little milestones every week. Every week I'd feel like I'd want to tell someone: 'Guess how far I swam/cycled/ran today?' Slowly, slowly, my confidence grew and I no longer thought I was going to die! I knew it was going to be the toughest thing I'd ever done, but … I was going to make it. His beautiful and patient wife had to endure me texting him every day with silly questions or proud timings for my training sessions.

No words can express how I feel about Greg. Just thinking about it makes me teary now… and I will never forget the way he got me across that lake, or through that last marathon.

He was the best mentor ever. Ever ever.

Davina McCall

John Bishop:
In 2012, when I agreed to take on the Sport Relief challenge, I was introduced to Professor Greg Whyte, who I was told would work with me to prepare for the event. In truth I totally underestimated how hard the 'Week of Hell' would be, but I also underestimated the influence Greg would have on me. Without him I would not have completed the challenge, as he was there literally every step of the way. But more importantly, without him I would not know myself as well as I do today.

His quiet authority is only matched by his determination that you will not fail. When Greg believes in you it is impossible not to believe in yourself, and you find strength you didn't know was there.

Few people in this life make you a better person, better than you ever thought you could be. Greg has that rare gift and we should all be grateful that he is willing to share it.

John Bishop

Kevin Cahill:
On a flight back from Ethiopia in 2005, David Walliams made the mistake of telling me that he had always wanted to swim the Channel. We were soon firmly on the case and he swam it the following year in ten hours – it was the first great Sport Relief challenge. Those challenges mix celebrity, jeopardy, common humanity and the feel-good factor in equal measure. It's a winning formula, make no mistake. Collectively they have now raised over £33 million, are loved by the nation and have changed countless lives at home and overseas.

One constant factor throughout them all has been the estimable Greg Whyte. He is a man of great compassion, loyalty and psychological strength. His failure to recognize the possibility of defeat is matched only by his dodgy sense of humour. We simply could not have done it without him. He is a fundraising and motivational god; we remain forever in his debt.

Kevin Cahill CBE
CEO, Comic Relief

CHAPTER ONE

THE SCALES OF SUCCESS

It always feels impossible until it has been achieved

'Nothing good comes easy' is a mantra I can often be heard saying to anyone considering a major challenge. Think about the delivery of a goal as a journey along a road from the point at which you decide on your goal, the vision, to the point of successfully achieving your goal, the delivery. This *road to success* is built on the foundations of hard work. In this book I will outline the journey along the *road to success* in pursuit of your goals, and while this provides the most direct route, one truth remains: success cannot exist without hard work.

Committing to working hard to achieve your goal is the first and most important step on your *road to success*. Unfortunately, the relationship between effort and reward is not linear. As you move closer to achieving your goal you will be required to work harder and harder to continue to progress. This law of diminishing returns often limits performance and, ultimately, success. On the plus side, the harder you work, the greater the reward. So don't let the fear of hard work halt you from taking the first step and committing to a challenge, but do recognize that you will achieve nothing of value without hard work.

Having established the absolute requirement for hard work in the *delivery of success* you must consider other factors that limit success. These limits to success impact on every step of your journey along the *road to success* from vision to delivery. The limits are the same in every aspect of life and they affect us all to varying degrees. For example, the limits that exist for elite athletes are exactly the same as those that exist for anyone taking on a major challenge. The barriers that Olympians have to negotiate to become champions are the barriers you too have to overcome, whether you are attempting to lose weight, improve your health, increase your productivity or swim the English Channel.

Limits to success can be divided into four main domains: Body, Mind, Technical and Environment. It is important to remember that these limits to success are, in the main, barriers to performance that can be negotiated. By creating solutions you will be able to overcome the limits and deliver success, leading to my most important mantra: 'Anything is possible'.

By the end of this chapter you will have gained an understanding of:

- The law of diminishing returns
- The Mountain of Success
- The limits of human athletic performance
- The four key factors limiting performance:
  - The Body (The Physical Self)
  - The Mind (The Psychological Self)
  - The Technical
  - The Environment
- How technology helped James Wood's Channel swim (challenge highlight)
- The barriers to success
- The *scales of success*
- How creating solutions for the levels of performance enabled the *This Morning* Channel swim (challenge highlight)

In each chapter of this book I will also be highlighting examples of extraordinary challenges I have been privileged to be part of over the years. These challenges include high-profile events for Sport Relief and Comic Relief as well as a variety of televised, individual and personal challenges. In this chapter, the challenge highlights focus on swimming the Channel.

THE HAPPY BANK

Throughout this book there is one component of success that transcends all others: HARD WORK. Nothing good comes easy, and therefore you should be prepared to invest the effort required to deliver success. I like to use the analogy of a personal bank account held at the 'Happy Bank'. Hard work is the currency that you invest in your account at the Happy Bank, which you can then withdraw at a later date along your *road to success*. When you invest time, effort or resource into your challenge, make a note of the investment. While you could make a simple mental note of your investment, I suggest that you write it down and calculate your total investment on a regular basis. This accounting task, rather than being an annoyance, is a fantastic way of monitoring your progress, which can act as an excellent reward and motivation for your efforts.

In sport there are a number of different systems that quantify training volume and which take into account how long and how hard the athlete has worked. You can construct your own system of investment measurement for every *determinant of success* (see Chapter 3 – The Wheel of Success). For example, if your challenge is weight management, you could use the following investment plan for physical activity:

Investment = duration of exercise × intensity (hard = 5 points; moderate = 3 points; easy = 1 point)

So, for example, if you go for three 30-minute easy walks and two hard 20-minute runs in a week you will invest the following:

Three easy 30-minute walks = 3 × (30 × 1) = 90 points
Two hard 20-minute runs = 2 × (20 × 5) = 200 points
Total investment for the week = 200 + 90 = 290 points

The more you invest in your Happy Bank account, in other words the harder you work, the greater the amount of happiness you can withdraw throughout your challenge. This is particularly important during those difficult periods when your belief, commitment and motivation (see more in Chapter 4 – The Brain of Success) will be placed under pressure. Remember, hard work is fundamental to success. However, it is the same hard work wisely invested into your Happy Bank account that will support your challenge and optimize your delivery of success.

THE LAW OF DIMINISHING RETURNS

There is one simple rule when it comes to performance enhancement: the better you get, the harder you have to work to improve. The relationship between improvement in performance and effort is not linear. In fact, it tends to be curvilinear, with the greatest improvements in performance occurring in the early stages followed by diminishing rewards for your hard work as you begin to progress. This is 'the law of diminishing returns'.

This law applies to every aspect of life. Think about dieting. Losing weight in the first few weeks is easy – the pounds just drop off with little effort and only minor changes in lifestyle (diet and physical activity). Unfortunately, this initial dramatic reduction in weight does not continue and it becomes increasingly difficult to shed those pounds. In order to achieve further weight loss you have to work harder, making significant changes to your diet and physical activity. This is invariably the point of failure for most people aiming to reduce weight and maintain that ideal weight over time.

Large reductions in weight, much like big improvements in physical performance, are highly rewarding in the early stages. However, as it begins to get harder to achieve goals, you are in danger

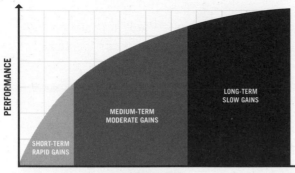

The Law of Diminishing Returns. Short, rapid gains in performance are followed by slower improvements in performance despite a greater input of effort. Finally, as you reach the performance necessary to deliver your goal, the long-term gains in performance require a significantly greater investment of effort over a much longer period of time.

of losing belief, motivation and commitment. That's why most diet plans only last six to twelve weeks and why New Year resolutions are cast on the scrapheap before spring has sprung! Keep in mind that you will have to continue working hard and that will help keep you on the *road to success*, through to the delivery of your goal.

THE MOUNTAIN OF SUCCESS

Armed with an understanding of the law of diminishing returns you are now in a better position to plan your journey along the *road to success*. Think about reaching your goal as a long road into the mountains, with early stages on the flat leading to the foothills, before the major ascent to the summit. You will travel a large distance making significant gains in performance on the flat road with limited effort. As you reach the foothills you will have to put more effort in to continue to improve performance. However, it is not until you reach the mountain road, close to achieving your goal, that you will have to work significantly harder, making much slower progress than earlier in your challenge. It may seem close, but you still have some distance to travel, and a common mistake is to underestimate the size of the final few steps.

Rather than take a direct route up the mountain, you will also

The Mountain of Success. Early progress is rapid with limited effort along flat roads, which leads to a reduced speed of progression in the foothills, finishing with a much slower rate of progression along the mountain roads leading to the *delivery of success.*

almost certainly have to follow a winding route with switchbacks to traverse the very steep sections and ensure you continue to improve your performance. This makes for slow progress despite significant effort. Planning your route prior to starting your journey is important in terms of understanding how much work is required and to ensure you remain focused on delivering your goal when the going gets tough. However, it is also important to remember that the best-laid plans may need a bit of tweaking in the light of new information.

THE LIMITS OF HUMAN ATHLETIC PERFORMANCE

In every chapter of this book I will explore some science to help explain and support some of the key concepts. I hope that you will indulge me on these brief sojourns into the field which has guided my thinking over the past three decades. Equally, I hope you find them both interesting and informative.

In the field of sport there is evidence that humans are reaching the limits of performance. World records continue to be set, but the improvements in performance are getting smaller. In addition, the time between the setting of new records is increasing, with some

800m RUNNING WORLD RECORDS

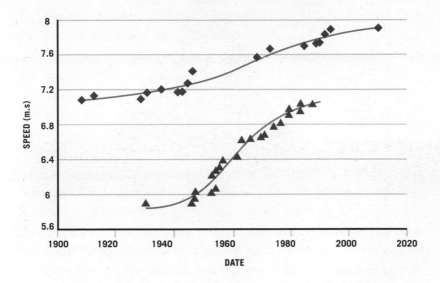

100m FREESTYLE SWIMMING WORLD RECORDS

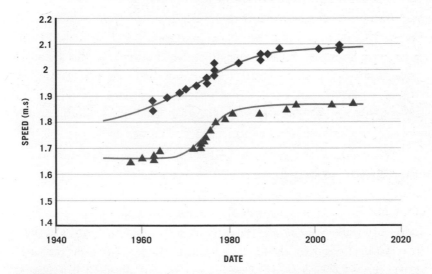

World records for 800m running and 100m freestyle swimming for both men (◆) and women (▲). Note: the plateauing of world-record speeds; the difference between men and women; and the most rapid increases in world-record speeds took place during the 1960s, 1970s and early 1980s.

records standing for decades before being broken. Along with colleagues, I have demonstrated that running and swimming world records are reaching a plateau for both men and women (men are consistently 10% faster than women across all events primarily due to physiological differences), suggesting that we are reaching the limits of human performance.

It is interesting to note that world records are not broken in a linear (straight line) fashion. The breaking of world records varies across time due to changes in a number of limits to performance. The fastest rate of increase in world-record performances occurred during the 1960s, 1970s and early 1980s. The reason for the rapid improvement in times during this period is likely to be associated with a number of factors which reduced the limits to performance. These include the advent of sports science and sports medicine, improved coaching science, improved facilities, the professionaliza-tion of sport and performance-enhancing drugs. While these areas of advancement may appear sport specific, each of these factors, with the exception of performance-enhancing drugs, can be translated into performance in all areas of life from health to business.

The limits of human athletic performance are the same as those that limit success in all areas of our lives. By understanding these limits we can create solutions and enhance our ability to deliver success. The four primary limits to success are the body, the mind, technical and the environment.

THE BODY OF SUCCESS

Our physical capabilities impact on all areas of life performance and not solely those we naturally relate to physical activity. Physical limitations are obviously closely linked to success in major physical challenges. Less obvious is the importance of physical limitations in the business arena or in terms of our quality of life; however, it is clear that physical capacity is linked with areas such as academic success, weight management and productivity. In other words, optimizing our physical self will reduce the limitations to performance across all areas of life.

Understanding the component parts of physical limitations enables us to profile ourselves against a 'gold standard' target and in doing so establish plans which optimize our physical self by targeting weaknesses and maintaining strengths. Some areas of our physical self are genetically set, for example our height. We are unable to impact on these areas; however, that does not mean we are limited by them, it simply means we have to find solutions to overcome the limitation. The vast majority of physical capabilities are modifiable, and as such we are able to continually improve our physical self and reduce the impact of this limit to performance.

THE MIND OF SUCCESS

Having the physical ability is not in itself enough to ensure success. Our minds play a central role in performance, so much so that a new sphere of psychology has recently emerged: performance psychology. Whether it is losing weight, creating a better-performing business or taking on a major physical challenge, optimizing psychological performance is critical. Some of the most important psychological limitations are belief, commitment and motivation (see Chapter 4 – The Brain of Success). If we are to overcome psychological factors that limit performance, and deliver success, we must optimize our psychological self. The psychological limits to success can often be greater than any physical, technical or environmental limit.

One of the best examples of psychological limits to performance was demonstrated on 6 May 1954, when Sir Roger Bannister became the first man to run below four minutes for a mile. Numerous attempts had been made, by the world's best athletes, to break the four-minute barrier but the target had remained elusive, and was even deemed impossible by many in both athletics and the media. To further cement the psychological barrier, it was believed by the medical and scientific community at the time that if a man ran below four minutes for a mile, he would die! This led to the famous quote from Bannister following his record-breaking run: 'Doctors and scientists said that breaking the four-minute mile was impossible, that one would die in the attempt. Thus, when I got up from the track after collapsing at the finish line, I figured I was dead.'

The psychological barrier had been overcome, and the record lasted only forty-six days: it was beaten by Bannister's great Australian rival John Landy by two seconds! The record now stands at 3:43.13 – seventeen seconds below the limit where death was considered the only outcome.

THE TECHNICAL OF SUCCESS

Technical limits to performance cover a range of limits to success from tactical and logistical decision-making to technological issues. This is best demonstrated when a technological breakthrough leads to advancements in performance. Technology can improve performance in a variety of ways. The most obvious role for technology is in reducing the time taken to perform tasks. High-performance sport presents clear examples of technologically related enhancements in speed, ranging from Mondo© track surfaces to anti-wave lane ropes in the pool.

Not only can technology improve existing performance, it can also allow performance where once it did not exist. As Director of Research for the British Olympic Association I had the pleasure of working with the British Paralympians. The role of technology in reducing the limits of performance in this group of elite athletes is clear to see. For example, specially designed prostheses using state-of-the-art materials have allowed amputees to travel at extraordinary speeds.

But it is outside the elite athlete environment where one of my best examples of the association between technology and performance overcame the limits of performance to deliver success.

Challenge Highlight

In 2010, I trained James Wood, the first European paraplegic to swim the English Channel. Maintaining core body temperature is one of the key determinants of success for cold open-water swimming: water is twenty-five times more conductive than air! For paraplegics, the large surface area of the legs with minimal muscle mass is a perfect radiator of heat, which leads to rapid and life-threatening cooling of the body. Overcoming this limit to success is achieved with technology: the wetsuit. Wetsuits are not a recent invention, but the new suits specifically designed for long-distance swimming have eliminated the limitations to open-water swimming. With his specially designed wetsuit, and after fourteen hours and twenty minutes, James reached the French shore and demonstrated the role of technology in overcoming the limits to success and allowing the *delivery of success*.

www.achievetheimpossible.co.uk

James Wood, the first European paraplegic to swim the English Channel.

THE ENVIRONMENT OF SUCCESS

The environment into which we are born and in which we live creates limits to performance in a range of ways that can result in fundamental limits to success. These environmental (sociological) limits include factors such as social class, affluence, ethnicity, where we live and who we live with. The impact of some environmental limits to success are overt. For example, affluence (how much money we have) can have a direct impact on success. The requirement for investment in a major project is often a requirement in the *delivery of success*; but that does not mean that the more money you have the more successful you will be. The fact that you do not have the perceived financial requirements does not immediately quash your ability to deliver success. By attracting investors of money (sponsors) and time (volunteers), reducing your costs and targeting your investment you will find that *anything is possible*.

In contrast, some environmental barriers to success are less obvious, for example social class or ethnicity. An example of social-class barriers can most readily be found in sport. In the early twentieth century the Victorian middle classes decided it was unfair that working-class athletes were beating them in the sporting arena. Accordingly, they banned the awarding of prize money and established amateur sport (with, for instance, the Amateur Athletic Association, or AAA). In doing so the Victorians closed access to sport for the working class who laboured six days per week and relied on income in the form of prize money to compete. The record books were re-set, and so began the era of amateur sport, which was the status quo into the mid-1980s.

Sadly, many of these environmental limits still exist in modern life; however, they are barriers which can be overcome. The only sociological limits to success are those we set ourselves.

BARRIERS TO SUCCESS

The *road to success* for any major challenge will be littered with barriers which have the potential to limit success. Hoping for the best and ignoring the barriers to success is almost certain to result in failure. Taking your chances and hoping that you will be able to clear or go around these barriers when they arise is also a recipe for disaster. Identifying the barriers and creating solutions to overcome them is fundamental to any successful journey.

If you can't get over them you will have to go around them

The limits to performance often present themselves as barriers which must be negotiated if we are to be successful. As we have seen, there are different types of limits and therefore barriers to performance. Establishing the nature of the barrier is important in understanding how we can overcome it. Some barriers are essential prerequisites for success which must be tackled and negotiated. For example, if you are looking to lose weight you must reduce your calorie consumption and increase your physical activity. You will not be able to successfully lose weight until you have tackled and overcome these barriers.

In contrast, there are some barriers that can be circumnavigated by creating a path around them. These paths do not ignore the barrier; they simply provide you with an alternative solution that allows you to continue along your *road to success*. For example, on a multi-day ultra-endurance challenge, navigation may be an important determinant of success for which you are ill-equipped. Rather than clearing this barrier by spending months learning navigation skills, or allowing the barrier to end your challenge, the solution may be to go around, by appointing a team member who has navigational expertise, or purchasing specialist equipment that can perform much of the task for you. Alternatively, if your challenge is to start an exercise programme as part of improving your health but you are lacking motivation, you could find an exercise buddy or appoint a personal trainer to provide extrinsic motivation until you become intrinsically self-motivated.

There are no problems, only solutions

Meticulous planning is fundamental to the *delivery of success*. Planning must include not only those factors which are required to deliver your goal – the determinants of success (see Chapter 3 – The Wheel of Success) – but also the barriers to success. By addressing the potential problems and planning a strategy to deliver solutions – an 'If–Then' plan (see Chapter 8 – The Delivery of Success) – you will be closer to creating an environment where there are no problems, only solutions. Finding the solutions to your barriers prior to starting will result in an uninterrupted journey along your *road to success*. In essence, you should prepare for the worst and then hope for the best.

Avoiding the potholes along the *road to success*

There are limits to success that are less predictable. I like to think of these as potholes as they can appear unexpectedly anywhere along the *road to success*. In these cases it is difficult to plan ahead and develop solutions. For example, you are preparing for a major physical challenge and are then unexpectedly called away to work abroad, where you know there are limited facilities for preparation. Also, it is not uncommon to socialize in the bar when on work trips – and so you go with the aim of training and end up boozing! As a result your goals halt and then you have the difficult task of restarting everything. Work trips may be a common occurrence, in which case it should not be a pothole but a barrier which you have planned for, and for which you have developed a solution. However, if this is an unusual request you will need to address it rapidly before the pothole opens up and becomes a chasm which will have a significant impact on performance.

Meticulous planning will reduce the number of potholes significantly and therefore reduce the limits to success. If you do hit a pothole, ensure that you use all the resources available to you, including your planned contingency, to make an informed decision which provides the best solution to the barrier in front of you. While speed is of the essence, it is important that you do not rush to a solution that may prove to be counterproductive in the long run. In providing the best solutions as quickly as possible the pothole becomes a barrier which can be overcome.

This process highlights the need for a flexible approach to planning with continual assessment of progress to ensure you take the most direct *road to success*. The best approach is to avoid the potholes altogether, though, so do not use potholes as an excuse for poor planning!

THE *SCALES OF SUCCESS*

Performance is a complex bio-social interaction of factors which must be understood and addressed if success is to be delivered. Ignoring the limits to performance is like applying the brakes along your *road to success*. You may make progress towards your goal but it will be slow-going and require a great deal more hard work than is necessary. The continual application of the brake will eventually lead to you running out of energy and slowing to a halt – and, ultimately, to failure.

Identifying and embracing the limits to success is the first step in identifying solutions to overcome the barriers. In order to deliver success you must balance the limits and solutions. This can be achieved by tackling the barriers head-on or identifying alternative strategies which allow you to circumnavigate the limit to performance. The most direct *road to success* will provide the quickest route to your goal; however, not all barriers can be addressed directly. Equally, trying to

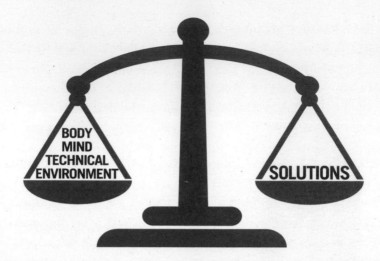

Scales of success. Your performance will be limited in four key areas: Body, Mind, Technical and Environment. Identifying solutions to overcome the barriers to success and establishing a balance will optimize your *delivery of success.*

go around every barrier is likely to result in very slow progress with a potential loss of belief, motivation and commitment, leading to failure. Finding the right balance of solutions which provides the smoothest *road to success* is likely to result in the quickest transit time. Once you have achieved balance on your *scales of success* you only need to focus on the potholes and ensure you make rapid, informed decisions to reduce their impact on your performance.

FROM SPORT TO LIFE

Much of my approach to delivering success has been developed around optimizing performance in elite sport, which I have taken into other areas of life. As athletes have moved closer to the limits of performance we have developed our understanding of how to continue advancing performance. This has been achieved across a variety of performance domains which include:

- Re-defining the limits of performance
- The advent and development of sports science and sports medicine
- The advent and development of coaching science
- The development of leadership
- The development of the team

In the following chapters I have translated these performance domains into all areas of performance from major physical challenges to weight management, and from health to business. In re-defining the limits of performance we have eroded the barriers to success and made what was once thought of as impossible, possible. Chapter 2 – The Vision of Success – examines the importance of pushing the boundaries of performance, and the importance of goal setting in the *delivery of success*.

The advent and development of sport science and medicine has led to our increased understanding of the component parts of performance – the determinants of success. This is an important area in delivering success and one which will be addressed in detail in Chapter 3 – The Wheel of Success. In addition, through our increased understanding of performance we have dramatically altered our view of the pivotal role of the mind in delivering success. This fundamental limit to success will be covered in Chapter 4 – The Brain of Success. The advent and development of coaching science is related to our enhanced understanding of how to deliver success. The key elements of planning and preparation are the focus of Chapter 5 – The Road to Success.

The landscape of elite sport has changed dramatically in recent times. The *Chariots of Fire* imagery of an athlete-and-coach team has evolved into a highly developed group structure which includes a range of specialists integrated to form large inter-disciplinary teams. This model of teamwork has underpinned the development of elite performance and is central to the enhancement of performance in any major challenge. Chapter 6 – The Team of Success – will examine the identification, appointment and coordination of a team required in the *delivery of success*. Alongside our enhanced understanding of the complexities of creating a *team of success*, a parallel development of leadership is essential to ensure the translation of knowledge into practice. Chapter 7 – The Leadership of Success – will address the characteristics of successful leaders.

Chapter 8 – The Delivery of Success – focuses on the requirements in the final and most important stage of delivering your vision, and Chapter 9 – The Perfect Storm for Success – provides an overview of the strategy for reaching your long-term goal from vision to delivery.

The aim of this book is to move people from the ordinary to the extraordinary, to make the seemingly impossible, possible.

Challenge Highlight

In the autumn of 2006, a researcher from the television show *This Morning* called to discuss the possibility of me training four women to take on a major swimming challenge. Having successfully trained David Walliams to swim across the English Channel on 4 July that year (a challenge we will look at in more detail in Chapter 4 – The Brain of Success), the team at *This Morning* had the vision of four women replicating this iconic feat.

For an experienced ultra-endurance swimmer a large number of limits exist for a successful swim across the Channel. These limitations are responsible for the low success rate across what is recognized as the 'blue riband' event of open-water swimming. Somewhere in the region of only four in every ten swimmers to attempt the crossing are successful. The reasons for this are many; however, once the swimmer has developed the physical capacity to swim non-stop for over twenty miles, the principal impediment is nature. Factors including the cold (the water temperature in the Channel peaks at 17°C in September), the tides (their speed, particularly spring tides, can be disastrous for a tiring swimmer) and the weather (wind is the major enemy, leading to big swells which can debilitate even the strongest swimmers) are common reasons for failure, which is why the timing and weather forecast for attempted crossings are so important. More people have reached the summit of Everest than have successfully swum the Channel!

The four women selected for this challenge were not experienced ultra-endurance swimmers. In fact they were very inexperienced swimmers: three of the four were unable even to swim front crawl! At our first session they swam head-up breaststroke. (It is a very long way across the Channel swimming head-up breast-stroke; at some point you have to get your hair wet.) But being weak swimmers was the least of the barriers facing these four very special women. Each had a personal story which would create unique limits that had to be tackled and overcome to deliver success.

My first swimmer was Pat, a fifty-nine-year-old great-grand-mother who as a child contracted tuberculosis which resulted in her losing her right hip, which was fused, leaving her with no movement in the hip. This creates a major limit to performance as the legs are crucial in balancing the body, particularly in open-water swimming. Second up was Sally, who had suffered from post-natal depression which had led her to attempt suicide on a number of occasions. Third was Lynne, whose son had died at the age of seven months; she was still struggling to deal with the tragedy. Finally there was Mel, who at the age of thirty-six had been diagnosed with breast cancer which led to a single mastectomy and a prolonged period of chemotherapy and radiotherapy. While the personal stories are in themselves major limits to performance, it is worth noting that for Lynne and Mel these life-changing events had occurred within two years of the challenge.

You would not be alone in thinking that the limits to perfor-mance associated with swimming the Channel combined with the personal histories of these women would make this an impossible challenge. However, understanding the determinants of success and recognizing the barriers to success, I planned an individually tailored strategy to deliver success. With a targeted preparation phase providing solutions to the barriers to performance and optimizing each determinant of success, the four women arrived in Dover harbour just thirty weeks after starting out on their seemingly impossible journey. But this was not the end of the limits to performance: now they had to deliver.

The day of the swim presented another not uncommon limit to success: the weather. It was blowing a force 6 gale with a twenty-foot swell (waves as tall as a house!). The women were about to face the toughest conditions in which it is safe to swim.

Having identified the limits of success, planned for all barriers to success and designed solutions to overcome them, the four women

Legends of the sea. Pat Nelson, Sally Ludlow, Mel Redding and Lynne Gilfellon successfully swam the Channel after just thirty-three weeks of preparation.

set out on their relay of one-hour rotations. Following a dedicated period of hard work, increasing as they progressed towards their goal, combined with a strategy that was meticulously tailored, and surrounded by a truly outstanding team, the four women touched French soil after thirteen hours and fifty-four minutes. The impossible had become possible.

▲ *www.achievetheimpossible.co.uk*

TASK
- Think about the challenge you have always wanted to achieve but thought was impossible.
- Write down the limits to achieving this goal under the following headings:
  - Body
  - Mind
  - Technical
  - Environment
- Identify and write down the solutions to these limits and construct your *scales of success* to ensure you have achieved a balance.

CHAPTER TWO

THE VISION OF SUCCESS

The SMART way to achieve your goals

Children constantly challenge themselves to prove that they can achieve something they or others think they cannot, or to compete against their contemporaries. This constant challenge is the way in which children develop, learn new skills and push the boundaries of their capabilities. Sadly, for many this drive to challenge ourselves is often lost with age.

There are a host of reasons why we fail to challenge ourselves as adults. Personal beliefs often lead to the thinking that we do not have the capabilities to succeed. In addition, we are all too often limited by what those around us think. Lack of belief from our family, friends and colleagues can create the barriers to challenge and success. This lack of belief results in a 'fear of failure' which often outweighs our desire for success. In this environment our default position is to maintain the status quo and not challenge ourselves.

It is clear that in order to push the boundaries of our capabilities beyond the expectations of ourselves and others we must have the vision to challenge ourselves by moving outside our comfort zone. Nothing great has ever been achieved from the sofa. We must be audacious in setting our challenge to ensure it is meaningful. Setting an audacious goal is the first step; but delivering success does not happen by chance. Understanding the journey along your *road to success* begins with setting a challenge that passes the three questions of destiny – importance, time and resources – in your Flow of Success.

Having established your challenge, the next step along your journey is to understand goal setting using the SMART Flow, and how to construct your Profile of Success. With these initial steps along your *road to success* in place you will be ready to move forward to identify the determinants of success.

By the end of this chapter you will have gained an understanding of:

- The fact that success is not a chance event
- The questions of destiny in your Flow of Success when committing to your vision
- The structure and function of short-, medium- and long-term goals
- Goal setting using the SMART approach
- How to use the SMART Flow to structure your goals
- How Christine Bleakley got SMART before water-skiing across the Channel (challenge highlight)
- How to construct your Profile of Success
- The vision behind comedian Eddie Izzard's forty-three marathons in fifty-one days (challenge highlight)

SUCCESS IS NOT A CHANCE EVENT

Success is never guaranteed; if it was, it wouldn't be a challenge. Equally, success doesn't happen by chance. Delivering success when taking on a major challenge is not like entering your numbers into the lottery. You cannot rely on chance to deliver success; if you do, you are likely to be as successful as you are at winning the lottery. When we embark on a major challenge we always look to predict outcome. Indeed, it is not uncommon to see a greater investment of time in predicting outcome compared to the planning, preparation and delivery of a challenge. Accompanied by hard work, the *delivery of success* is wholly reliant upon a carefully and meticulously structured process which is underpinned by a number of important steps delivered along a defined path: the *road to success*. Remember, the best way to predict success is to create it.

BIG IS BEAUTIFUL

The boundaries of our capabilities are rarely governed by fact. All too often our abilities are dictated by our own beliefs or the beliefs of those around us. How often have you thought about doing something challenging and found yourself saying, 'But I'll never be able to achieve that!' More often, in my experience, it is the condemnation of those closest to you, your family and friends, that plays the critical role in snuffing out a challenge before it has even begun. 'There's no way you can do that!' and 'Are you crazy?' are classic responses to the presentation of a potential challenge to friends and family that leads to the first and most important roadblock to success. Overcoming this first barrier is important and can only be achieved if you are armed with the right answers to the questions of destiny.

There are some challenges which you know are beyond your capabilities. For example, winning an Olympic gold medal in gymnastics in your fifties is implausible because of the inexorable decline in physiological factors such as aerobic capacity, strength and power. That doesn't mean winning an Olympic medal isn't possible in your fifties, though: a shooting medal, for instance, may be deliverable. Setting aside those challenges which are simply beyond your capabilities (and probably everyone in your position), never discount any challenge without first objectively assessing your potential to deliver success. My advice is simple: never be afraid to set an audacious goal. With meticulous planning, preparation and delivery, anything is possible.

QUESTIONS OF DESTINY

People often ask me, 'Have you ever rejected a challenge?', to which I reply, 'No.' Of course, there is a caveat to that answer. We have already spoken about the need to be audacious in our vision; however, the long-term goal, while being challenging, must be achievable. A challenge may not be achievable for a range of reasons and making sure you are being realistic is an important first step on the *road to success*. One of the main reasons for failure is the setting of unrealistic, unachievable goals. Setting a challenge should not be made on the spur of the moment. Making sure you fully evaluate the requirements of the challenge prior to committing to it is probably the most important step on your *road to success*.

There are three questions of destiny to answer:

1. Is the challenge important to me?
2. Do I have the time to commit to the planning, preparation and delivery of the challenge?
3. Do I have the resources to deliver success?

IS IT REALLY THAT IMPORTANT?

Answering 'Yes' to this question is fundamental to the success of the challenge. 'Maybe' or 'Somewhat' are not sufficient. As I will emphasize throughout this book, the *road to success* is built on the foundations of hard work. In order to ensure your commitment to hard work a 'Yes' response to the importance question is a prerequisite of success. And please note, the question is *not* if the challenge is important – most challenges are important – it is whether it is important to *you*.

During the preparation and delivery of the project there will be 'dark' moments when you question why you are doing the challenge and whether you can go on. If the challenge is not important to you, it will invariably be left in jeopardy. As we will discuss in Chapter 4 – The Brain of Success, the cornerstone of belief, commitment and motivation is the importance of the challenge to you. We can manipulate time and resources, but success will be very difficult to deliver without importance.

You can increase the importance of a challenge in a number of ways. For example, in business you can incentivize with rewards, monetary or otherwise. For major physical challenges, raising money for a charity with a personal meaning can raise the importance of a challenge dramatically. In order for rewards to raise the overall importance of a challenge the rewards must also be important to you. For example, paying somebody more money may not be important enough to them to have a significant impact on the response to this question of destiny.

One of the main reasons people struggle with the importance of a challenge is that they have competing goals, and they don't realize these goals are in competition – for example, someone who likes food but wants to lose weight, or athletes who feel guilty when training because they are not spending time with their family. During the 'dark times', these competing goals present conflicting messages which can lead to the slowing down, or possible ending, of a challenge. Ensuring that the challenge is important is the first step in establishing an achievable goal.

TIME WAITS FOR NO MAN

One of the commonest excuses I hear for failing to take on a major challenge is 'I haven't got the time'. My response is usually the same as the advice my dad used to give me: 'You've got to make time!' This might appear a little condescending but it has a ring of truth about it. For most of us the absence of time is not because we are busy – which is invariably true for all of us – it's usually the result of two factors: poor time management and poor communication.

Time waster

One of the most interesting experiments you will ever undertake on yourself is to monitor how much unproductive time you spend throughout a week. Just try it for a day. Using the stopwatch on your smartphone, time all the periods in a day that you could use for something more productive. Nothing should be off limits; home, work and leisure time should all be scrutinized. Travel can be one of the biggest drains on your time so think carefully about how you can use this time more productively. Could you structure your day more efficiently to free up time? How much time do you spend on coffee and lunch breaks? Could you extend your day by getting up a little earlier (you could go to bed earlier to make up for lost sleep rather than watch another rerun on Dave)? Be ruthless with your time experiment and see how much 'time you can make'.

It's good to talk

When considering taking on a major challenge you should first talk with your family to ensure that they share your commitment to the challenge and understand how much time is required to deliver success. This is a critically important conversation as the outcome will directly impact on your ability to prepare optimally for the challenge. Make sure you enter the conversation with a thoroughly researched and realistic plan of your time requirements. A common mistake is to underestimate the time commitment and mis-sell the challenge to your family. This can only lead to problems which will impact on your preparation.

Having agreed your time requirements with your family the next step is to inform your work and friends of your plan. Being supported by your family, friends and colleagues means that everyone has a greater understanding of the time you need to commit. This will make it much easier to set aside in your diary dedicated periods for preparation and reduce the potential conflict when people encroach on this time with other requests. It really is surprising how much time you can create just by sharing your vision.

MONEY, MONEY, MONEY . . .

Having the appropriate resources is important in the *delivery of success*. There are clear examples from elite sport that the more money you spend, the greater your return. Take a look at the Olympic medal table and you will see the dominance of those nations that invest the greatest amount of money. In fact, there is a linear relationship between investment and medals. Team GB's success at the London 2012 Olympic Games is an excellent example of the concept of return on investment. Team GB received a total funding of around £660 million and achieved a record-breaking third place on the Olympic medal table, beaten only by the sporting superpowers of the USA and China whose investment exceeded that of Team GB. Within Team GB itself the investment/medal relationship is best demonstrated by cycling, whose record haul of twelve medals (eight of them gold) was underpinned by an investment of over £26 million. Accordingly, the more you invest, the greater your likelihood of success. However, it's not that simple, as we will discuss in later chapters. Money is only valuable when it is used intelligently to deliver against an individually tailored, well-planned preparation and delivery. Just because it's expensive doesn't make it the best.

When you are establishing your resource goals you should ensure you follow the SMART principle, which I will come to shortly.

In addition to money, the absence of key resources will negatively impact on the *delivery of success*. For example, if you are intending to row the Atlantic you will need open-water (sea/ocean) training and experience. This doesn't mean you have to live on the coast but it may impact on the time and financial requirements which must be factored into the answers to your questions of destiny.

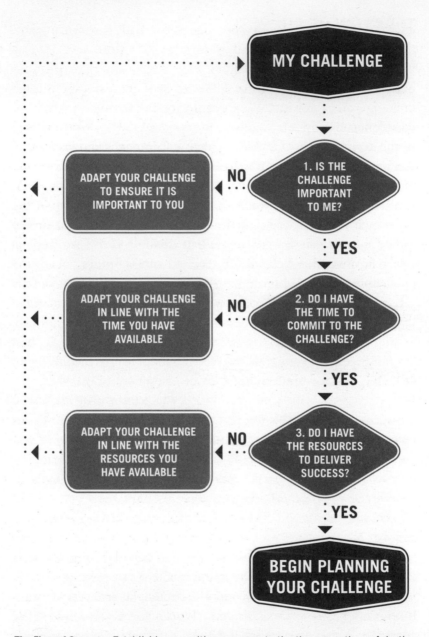

The Flow of Success. Establishing a positive response to the three questions of destiny is the first step on your *road to success.*

THE FLOW OF SUCCESS

The initial step in your journey requires you to answer the questions of destiny. Providing a positive answer to each of the questions is the only way you can ensure you are setting out on the right journey for you. A negative answer to any of the questions will ultimately lead to the construction of barriers which will impede your *delivery of success*. Follow the *flow of success* on page 46 to establish whether or not you are in a position to begin planning your challenge. As you will see from the flow diagram, answering 'No' to any of the three questions does not mean the end of your journey; it simply indicates the requirement to re-evaluate the challenge. Having established whether changes can be made to the importance, time or resource requirements of the challenge you can re-enter the flow diagram on a circular basis until you have responded 'Yes' to all three questions.

SHOUT FROM THE ROOFTOPS

Once you have committed to a challenge with the support of your family, friends and colleagues, make sure you tell everyone you know or meet. Advertising your challenge provides an opportunity to market your challenge, garner support, enhance your self-confidence and ultimately improve your performance.

Marketing your challenge to the masses improves your chances of finding support. For example, finding specific expertise can sometimes be a minefield for the uninitiated. Sifting through a list of potentials to differentiate the experts from the charlatans is made simpler by talking to a wider community. In business we call it 'tendering', or 'expressions of interest'. As a business you would never accept the first bid you receive, and the same should be true for any challenge. You also stand a better chance of attracting support for other determinants of success (as we will see in the next chapter), including financial, equipment, fundraising, etc.

One of the common mistakes I see is the hiding of challenges for fear of failure. The possibility that the project may not be successful is often used as a reason to tell nobody. Alternatively, the fear that someone may discourage you if you tell them can sometimes lead to a vow of silence. My advice is to take the opposite view and use others to provide additional support to enhance your confidence. It is important to select the people you tell carefully. Avoid telling those you know have a negative outlook on life or would be happy to criticize you. Such people will invariably offer little support for your challenge and could be detrimental to your *brain of success*. Select instead family, friends and colleagues who have a positive outlook on life and you can be much more confident in the support you will receive. There is nothing quite like somebody heaping praise on you for taking on a challenge or asking you how the challenge is progressing. In order to deliver success, your desire for success must outweigh your fear of failure. Using others to provide a reservoir of confidence that you can tap into, particularly at low points during the preparation for a challenge, can be incredibly uplifting.

YOU CAN'T EAT THE ELEPHANT IN ONE BITE!

Major challenges can often appear insurmountable when viewed as a whole. The key to delivering success is to dissect the challenge into a number of smaller steps which together make up the journey along your *road to success*. Each step can be viewed as a short-term goal. Combining a number of steps (short-term goals) leads to the delivery of a medium-term goal, and combining medium-term goals leads to the completion of your journey, the delivery of your long-term goal (your vision) and success. While the concept of goal setting appears simple, there are a number of rules which must be followed if you are to deliver success. These rules are encapsulated in the SMART principle, as follows:

S – specific, significant, stretching
M – measurable, meaningful, motivational
A – agreed upon, achievable, action-orientated
R – relevant, results-orientated, rewarding
T – timely, time-bound, trackable

THE 'S' IN SMART

When setting your goals you should be very *specific* about what you are trying to achieve. Focusing on one determinant of success with each goal makes it much simpler to measure. Rather than trying to cover a number of aspects of each determinant under a single goal, partitioning them into separate goals will help you focus on delivering your specific target outcome. As well as being specific, the goal should be *significant* in its contribution to achieving overall success. Your challenge should be important to you, so every goal, however small, should be important in moving you closer to the delivery of your long-term goal and success. In order to ensure that you are continually moving towards delivering success, your goals should be *stretching*. Make sure you design your goals to target a progressive improvement in each determinant of success.

THE 'M' IN SMART

You have to know when you have achieved your goal, therefore every goal must be *measurable*. Being able to objectively measure your goal allows you to clearly identify when you have succeeded. However, it may not be possible to objectively measure some goals. If your goal is to reduce your anxiety at work as part of your long-term goal to improve your health, for example, you can use a subjective rating which you clearly identify before you start working towards your goal. You could rate your anxiety on a 1 (not anxious) to 5 (very anxious) scale and continually assess your progress. Just as your long-term goal (your challenge) should be important to you, every goal should be *meaningful*. Every goal should take you a step closer to success. By reaching your goals you can clearly measure your progress which will provide a valuable source of *motivation* as you continue your journey along your *road to success* to your long-term goal.

THE 'A' IN SMART

It is important that you *agree* your goals before you set out on your journey. A lack of clear definition of your goals before starting will result in you meandering as you try to find your way. Your goals are your road map, without which you are much more likely to get lost. Every goal should be *achievable*, but they should also be challenging. By making goals too easy you will progress slowly, leading to a loss of motivation. By making goals too challenging, you are unlikely to achieve them. Your goals should direct you to take *action*. In other words, you must be required to work in order to achieve your goal; do not set goals for things that already exist.

THE 'R' IN SMART

Your goals must be *relevant* to your challenge. It is sometimes easy to set goals that, while appearing important, may not contribute to your determinants of success. All goals should be *results-orientated*. You must always look to achieve a pre-determined result, whether it is objective or subjective. Only accepting success when you have achieved your goal is the key to ensuring you make continual progress along your *road to success*. *Rewarding* yourself when reaching your goals is crucial to ensure you optimize your motivation. Recognizing success in attaining your short- and medium-term goals by rewarding yourself will provide a valuable psychological tool that can be used to maintain your commitment to the challenge.

THE 'T' IN SMART

You must think carefully about the order of your goals. They need to be *timely* – some goals need to be achieved before you progress to your next goal. A common reason for failing to achieve a goal is that you simply have not achieved the prerequisite goals. Your short- and medium-term goals must also be *time-bound* in order to ensure that you remain on track to deliver your long-term goals. Make sure you allot the appropriate amount of time to every goal. Giving yourself too much time can often lead to a loss of focus and too little time to deliver. *Tracking* your goals allows you to monitor your progress along your *road to success*. Continually tracking your progress will ensure you take the most direct route on your journey and avoid wasting time, effort and resources.

Challenge Highlight

In March 2010, TV presenter Christine Bleakley successfully water-skied across the Channel for Sport Relief. She was pulled at 30mph, and the crossing took one hour and forty minutes. The physical challenge of ultra-endurance waterskiing was compounded by the extreme environmental conditions: a water temperature of 5°C and an air temperature of 3°C resulted in significant wind chill and real dangers for both performance and health.

Christine had faced a number of limits to performance, physical, psychological and technical. Prior to embarking on this audacious goal she had never waterskied before, she lacked the strength and endurance required to waterski for twenty-one miles, and she couldn't swim! All of these limits resulted in a significant fear of failure and a negative impact on her *brain of success* (more

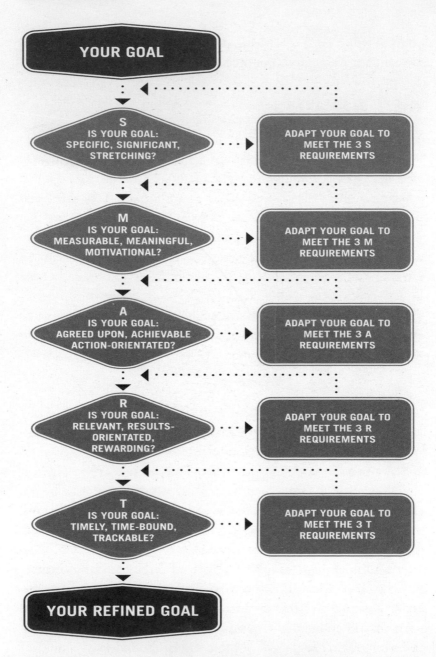

The SMART Flow. To ensure you optimize your goal setting you should ensure that your goal meets the SMART criteria. Working through the SMART Flow will help mould your goals to optimize your *delivery of success.*

Goal success. Christine Bleakley on the French shore having successfully waterskied twenty-one miles in an hour and forty minutes.

on this in Chapter 4 – The Brain of Success). Preparing for this challenge required meticulous goal setting focused upon each determinant of success. Using the SMART principle, we established short- and medium-term goals for physical and technical determinants which closely aligned with Christine's *brain of success*. By setting these goals, Christine was able to focus on challenging and achievable targets without becoming overwhelmed by the enormity of the long-term goal.

www.achievetheimpossible.co.uk

THE PROFILE OF SUCCESS

A goal usually signifies the successful end point of a period of hard work. As an analogy, think about a mountain stage on the Tour de France. The best approach is to partition the stage into smaller bite-sized chunks. By setting short- and medium-term goals you will be able to cope much better with the demands of the stage. As you are riding along your *road to success* (there will be more on this specifically in Chapter 5 – The Road to Success) you will be able to tick off a successful summit (short-term goal) or reaching a major intermediate milestone (medium-term goal), for instance halfway on the stage or one hour to the finish. Ticking off these key markers of success will provide reward and motivation, driving you on to the finish line and success.

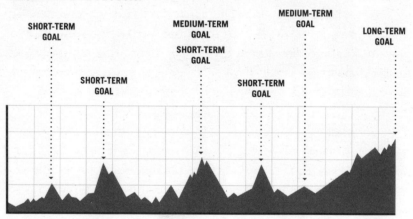

The Profile of Success. Your short-, medium- and long-term goals are like a series of hard climbs along your *road to success*.

CHARTING SUCCESS

Constructing a chart of your challenge including your short- and medium-term goals provides an important visual aid to demonstrate your progress as you move through the challenge. Make sure your chart is hung in a public space so that you and your family and friends can view it on a regular basis to reaffirm your successes. Ticking off goals as they are attained provides a visual motivational cue which will keep you focused on delivering to plan.

SMELL THE ROSES

Make sure you celebrate reaching every short- and medium-term goal by rewarding yourself. Writing down your rewards alongside your goals is a great motivational tool, particularly for those determinants of success you hate. Make sure the reward means something to you. You can use extrinsic or intrinsic rewards. Extrinsic rewards are prizes that you award yourself. The size of the award is not important as long as it has a significant meaning and provides positive affirmation of your success. A note of caution: make sure your extrinsic reward is appropriate to your challenge; avoid using rewards which have the potential to affect your challenge negatively. For example, if your challenge is to lose weight, avoid rewarding yourself with cakes!

Alternatively, you can seek to achieve intrinsic rewards such as pride, a sense of personal competence, high self-esteem, and that inner belief you possess when you have done something you really wanted to achieve. You do not receive a prize for these types of reward; rather you will take personal pride in your achievements. Allowing someone else to be the judge as to whether or not you have achieved the goal removes the temptation to cheat and adds value to the reward process as it becomes a prize-giving ceremony with public recognition of your achievement. It is very important that you do not reward yourself if you do not reach your goal. Only rewarding success is much more meaningful and empowering than constantly patting yourself on the back irrespective of success.

Challenge Highlight

One sunny morning in June 2009 I arrived at the Wolseley in central London for a breakfast meeting with Kevin Cahill, the CEO of Comic Relief, and the comedian Eddie Izzard. The purpose of the meeting was to discuss a major challenge for Sport Relief 2010. It was clear from the very start that Eddie had a vision of what he wanted to do. His first words to me were, 'Greg, I'm going to run around the UK.'

Following a brief discussion, during which I explained that the UK coastline stretches over 3,500 miles, we agreed that his plan might be problematic in the time frame available. Instead, I suggested that given a marathon is 42km we should perhaps look at forty-two marathons, visiting the cities where Eddie had lived as a child: London, Cardiff, Belfast and Edinburgh. Unfortunately, we were unable to design a course of forty-two marathons and had to add a forty-third to get him back to London for his finish on the steps of Trafalgar Square.

This idea didn't faze Eddie, but as we continued to talk it became clear how visionary this challenge was. On a number of levels this was truly an audacious goal. First, I asked Eddie, 'How much running have you done?'

'None,' came the response. This was not an exaggeration: Eddie didn't even own a pair of running shoes.

When I asked him what had given him the idea for the challenge he regaled me with a story about the previous day when he had decided to run from his hotel in central London to a meeting twenty-two miles away because he didn't want to drive! Having set off at eight a.m., he arrived at his meeting at six p.m., ten hours later. While this demonstrated Eddie's lack of running conditioning, it also provided evidence of his determination – a trait that was fundamental and one he had to depend on in order to complete his challenge.

Marathon man. Comedian Eddie Izzard ran forty-three marathons in fifty-one days despite never having run before (at all!).

The second key aspect of the challenge which made it audacious was time. In our discussions over breakfast it emerged that Eddie had to start the challenge in mid-July due to touring commitments in the autumn. This gave me only six weeks to prepare the challenge, the team and, of course, Eddie for what was to become one of the most iconic Sport Relief challenges of all time. This was truly a bold undertaking which was not going to be achieved by chance.

Eddie successfully completed all forty-three marathons in fifty-one days, clocking his fastest time (five hours and four minutes) on his final run. It was a true demonstration of the need for vision when designing a challenge and, as you will see in future chapters, an exemplar of the fact that success is not a chance event.

www.achievetheimpossible.co.uk

TASK
- Write down your vision.
- Research the answers to your questions of destiny.
- Using the Flow of Success, answer the questions of destiny.
- Mould your vision until you answer 'Yes' to all three questions of destiny.
- Make sure you understand the SMART principles in preparation for setting your goals after reading the next chapter, The Wheel of Success.

CHAPTER THREE

THE WHEEL OF SUCCESS

What is required to deliver success, and what are the risks?

In order to perform to the best of your ability you must have a clear understanding of what is required to deliver success. Performance is composed of a number of component parts which must all be optimized if you are to be successful. Dissecting a challenge into its individual determinants of success and profiling yourself against a desired 'gold standard' will allow you to establish your strengths and weaknesses. Creating a plan to deliver success cannot be achieved without developing a detailed understanding of what successful performance is made up of and what your personal profile looks like.

Having established the requirements to deliver success you must then analyse, in detail, the potential risks that may negatively impact on your performance. Developing an 'If–Then' plan to provide solutions should the potential risks become a reality is critical if you are to minimize impact on performance and optimize your chances of success.

By the end of this chapter you will have gained an understanding of:

- How to identify the determinants of success
- How to construct your *wheel of success*
- How to establish your own profile of strengths and weaknesses
- How to monitor your progress
- Charlie Pitcher's solo rowing record (challenge highlight)
- How to establish risks to performance
- How to develop an 'If–Then' plan to have the solution ready to overcome barriers and reduce the risks to performance
- John Bishop's 'Week of Hell' triathlon (challenge highlight)

ONE SMALL STEP FOR MAN . . .

Every journey begins with the first step, which for most of life's challenges is the initial commitment to take on the challenge. When it comes to the determinants of success, it is usually this first step where most of us fail, and it's not always due to our personal commitment. As we discussed in the previous chapter, we are often dissuaded by family, friends and colleagues from entering into a challenge. Worse still, we are told that it is impossible and we will never be able to achieve success. When we add the negative reinforcement from others to our own doubts, the usual response is to withdraw from the challenge before it has even begun. So, the first and possibly most important determinant of success is to commit to the challenge by taking the first step and entering. By entering into the challenge you are creating a contract with yourself to commit to the challenge and deliver a successful outcome.

It is important to note that entering a challenge is not enough to guarantee success, but if you don't do it, you will never know what it feels like to succeed!

While failing to enter due to self-doubt and negative reinforcement from others is common, it is the lack of forethought prior to entry that results in another major stumbling block to success. There are two major determinants of success that are fundamental to success: Time and Effort.

IF IT WAS EASY, EVERYONE WOULD BE DOING IT

There is no doubt that nothing good comes easy. This is particularly true of major physical challenges. Despite all of us acknowledging this fact, many believe that simply committing to a challenge is enough to be successful. Sadly, this is not the case. If a challenge is worth achieving it will definitely require a commitment to work hard. This is an inescapable truth, so if you know that you will not commit to working hard then you should seriously consider whether you should take on the challenge. The amount of work required for success is not dictated by how big the challenge is. It has much more to do with the journey required to achieve success. If you have never run before, or you are recovering from injury or illness, then taking on a 5km run can present the same challenge as an experienced ultra-endurance runner taking on the Marathon des Sables (a multi-day ultra-endurance race in the Sahara Desert – 'the toughest footrace on the planet').

In this chapter, I will be referring mainly to the field in which I have done some of my recent high-profile work, that of endurance challenges, but the lessons can be applied to almost any challenge you might take on. It is important to remember that every journey is personal. A common mistake is to assume that a challenge will be easy because a large number of people have successfully completed it before, or others have told you it is easy. This is true of major endurance challenges such as the marathon as well as all other major challenges, such as weight management, smoking cessation or business development. If a challenge is worth achieving then you can guarantee it will require a significant amount of effort.

YOU CAN'T TURN BACK THE CLOCK

Having the time to deliver the hard work is fundamental to success. You will need to have dedicated time to deliver the determinants of success. That means not only the time for the physical training but also the time required to deliver on all determinants of success. A common mistake is to get midway through the preparation for a major challenge and realize that you haven't got enough time to optimize each of the determinants of success.

It is important to predict how much time is required to deliver success before you enter into the challenge. If you are new to the challenge or have never taken on the specific major challenge before, it is always good to seek advice from experts in the area. And it is important to seek the best advice possible, which may mean an investment of time, maybe even a little money. A little investment at this point will mean big savings in time and money in the long run.

There are a number of ways of accessing the right advice, including the internet where you will find expert opinion from a range of sources (often the organizer's website has some of the best information which is specific to the event). Try not to underestimate the time required to do this research; it always takes more time than you think, so you need patience. Accurately predicting the time commitment is so important to planning your route to achieving your goal. If you get it right, you will be able to better structure your life around the challenge and, importantly, your family, friends and work colleagues will have a clear understanding of your commitment which will manage expectations and reduce potential conflict. Having established how much time you will need and deciding whether you are able to commit is critical to the delivery of a successful challenge and avoiding the common mistake of believing that you can create time or you can make up for lost time later in your preparation – it never happens!

Ask the expert

Talking to those who have completed the challenge before can be valuable, but a word of caution: prior participation does not an expert make. Plus, their journey may have been very different from yours, in terms of their previous experience, their time availability, their definition of success, etc. A common mistake is to talk to too many people, most of whom are not experts: the internet is flooded with views, many of which are not trustworthy. Invariably, talking to a large number of people leads to a host of conflicting views and recommendations which only serve to create confusion in your own mind. So it is very important to seek the best advice possible and use them as a sounding board to filter advice from other sources. This will lead to the best advice tailored to your needs.

EXAMINE EVERY ASPECT OF PERFORMANCE IN DETAIL

Having committed to the challenge and created a contract with yourself, agreeing to work hard and create the time required to deliver success, the next step is to identify the determinants of success. Every performance is multi-faceted, requiring the optimization of each determinant of success to ensure success. The number of determinants will be associated with the specific demands of the challenge. Some determinants, like the route, will not be important to challenges where courses are marked; however, for challenges where the course is not prescribed, route planning is a critical determinant of success.

Many different challenges may share the same determinants of success, such as physical preparation, but, as we will see later in the chapter, the detailed breakdown of the determinant may be vastly different depending on the nature of the challenge. Taking time to establish the determinants of success at the start of the project will save you time, effort and money in the long run. A common mistake is to rush or ignore this element of planning which often results in a last-minute panic to redress the shortfall in preparation. Having established the determinants of success you can then construct your *wheel of success*.

A PICTURE TELLS A THOUSAND WORDS

My personal preference is always to use diagrammatic representations when it comes to profiling and monitoring the determinants of success. By using a diagram you can quickly and easily identify areas of strength and weakness and track how they change throughout a challenge. Having established your determinants of success you can now apply them to your *wheel of success*.

The next important step is to clearly define 'success', as this will provide you with your principal goal (an area we covered in detail in Chapter 2 – The Vision of Success). Defining what you consider success to be, whether it is winning a challenge or simply crossing the finish line, will alter the goals for each of the determinants of success.

Having established your principal goal, you now need to decide your scoring system for your *wheel of success*. There are very simple and very complex ways to achieve this. When presenting the determinants as an overall score you can use a straightforward 5-point approach as follows:

0 = None
1 = Poor
2 = Average
3 = Good
4 = Excellent

Being able to 'anchor' your measurement criteria is crucial to optimizing the value of your *wheel of success*. 'Anchoring' is simply understanding what your point 0 and point 4 mean in reality. Generally, it is a simple task to anchor the lower end of the scale as most of us start a challenge at 0 for the vast majority of determinants of success. It is possible that certain determinants such as physical and psychological performance may be much more advanced. In contrast, the most difficult point to anchor is 4. What does excellence look like?

The answer to this question is, in part, personal; however, seeking expert advice is valuable to ensure that your definition of

'Excellent' is appropriate for a successful outcome. A common mistake is to underestimate or overestimate the requirements for excellence, and that is largely led by personality. If you are a perfectionist you will tend to ask too much of yourself to attain a grade 4. Alternatively, if you are a bit too laissez-faire you will veer towards underestimating the excellence score. Both positions are problematic as they will lead to underperformance for different reasons. Once you have anchored the bottom and top of your scale you can add as many grades between as you see fit; but, for the overarching determinants of success, keep it simple.

Having established your determinants of success and anchored your grading scale for each of the determinants you are now in a position to profile yourself against these criteria.

Below is an example of a *wheel of success* using a 5-point

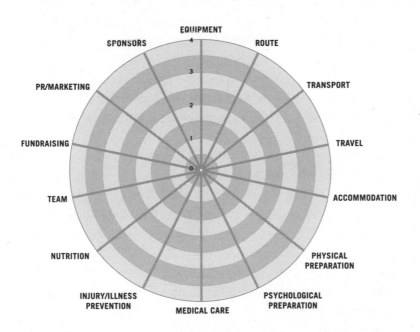

The *wheel of success* based upon the determinants of success with a 5-point grading scale ranging from 0 (None) to 4 (Excellent) against which you will profile yourself and plot a rating.

scoring system for a multi-day, single-discipline challenge for which, in addition to the standard determinants (physical preparation, nutrition, and so on), there are also specific determinants such as transport.

PROFILE-PRESCRIBE-MONITOR

Having established the *wheel of success* you can follow a very simple but effective circular approach to delivering excellence. The starting phase is profiling yourself against your scoring system to establish your strengths and weaknesses. The next phase is prescription, where you intervene to make positive change to the determinant; this could be the process of identifying team members, or constructing a training programme and starting physical training. The final phase is monitoring, which requires a re-profiling of your performance against your scoring system and identifying changes on your *wheel of success*.

This process is continuous until you have reached grade 4 to ensure you remain excellent while working on other determinants to deliver a wheel of excellence (where all determinants are graded

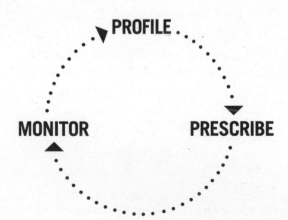

The circle of Profile-Prescribe-Monitor, a continuous process which provides a profile of strengths and weaknesses and a targeted intervention to create a wheel of excellence.

as 4). This circle of Profile-Prescribe-Monitor is therefore constantly refreshing itself from one phase to the next.

PROFILE: ESTABLISHING YOUR STRENGTHS AND WEAKNESSES

Having established your determinants of success, the next phase is to identify where you are in relation to each determinant based on your grading system. It is important to be as objective as possible when grading yourself; however, some areas will require elements of subjective appraisal as it may be difficult to measure and quantify every aspect of the determinant. For example, when grading your team determinant you can quantify the number of team members and their specific skills but it is very difficult to objectively measure how they will cope under pressure or interact with each other if they are new to the challenge.

A common mistake is to assume that these difficult-to-quantify aspects cannot be assessed. In order to optimize your chance of success you should create ways to measure every aspect of performance to enable you to make appropriately prescribed interventions to enhance performance. Replicating parts of the challenge which are likely to be difficult will give you some idea of how your team will cope under pressure. For example, on multi-day challenges, sleep deprivation is a major cause of team conflict, so it is worth running some overnight sessions inducing sleep deprivation and monitoring how the team copes and who or what is likely to be the catalyst for conflict. By doing this you put yourself in a better position to grade your team performance on your *wheel of success*.

Overleaf is an example of a *wheel of success* following the initial profiling. It is clear to see areas of weakness and relative strengths which allow you to prescribe interventions to bring about positive change.

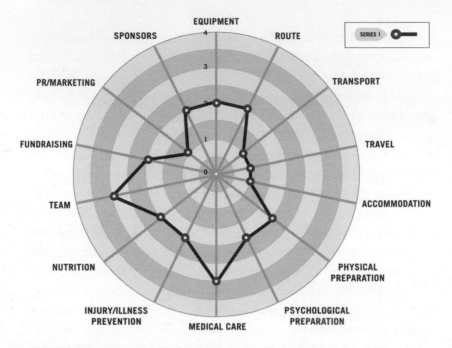

Profiling. The initial stage of developing each of the determinants of success comes from establishing your current ranking on each determinant. The *wheel of success* provides a pictorial representation of your strengths and weaknesses giving immediate visual feedback.

PRESCRIBE: TAILORED INTERVENTIONS TO POSITIVELY IMPACT ON EACH DETERMINANT OF SUCCESS

Having identified your strengths and weaknesses, the next phase is to prescribe interventions tailored specifically to meet your requirements and those of the challenge. The culmination of all the interventions is placed under the umbrella of preparation and will be covered in more detail in Chapter 5 – The Road to Success. The focus of the tailored prescription under each determinant of success is to bring about positive changes in all areas of performance. Some key determinants – physical and psychological performance – will require continual prescription whereas others – travel, for instance

– may only require discrete prescription at certain times according to progress in other determinants and based upon the overall plan for the challenge.

Having tailored interventions in each determinant of success, the next phase is to monitor (re-profile) progress based upon your *wheel of success*.

MONITOR: MEASURE PROGRESS TO ENSURE YOU ARE MOVING IN THE RIGHT DIRECTION

The monitoring process is simply a re-profiling of your determinants of success; however, there are a number of key issues regarding the timing of monitoring and the subsequent prescription.

The timescale for monitoring each of the determinants is likely to be different based upon the nature of the intervention. Planning the duration of time between profiling and re-profiling is important. By monitoring too soon you are unlikely to observe any meaningful change, which can lead to a loss of motivation associated with lack of progress which will impact on your belief, commitment and motivation (see Chapter 4 – The Brain of Success). By monitoring over too long a timescale you are likely to become anxious regarding your progress or spend too long focusing on a small number of determinants at the expense of other determinants. It can be a simple task to establish appropriate timescales for the monitoring of some determinants (travel). For other determinants (physical performance), it may be more difficult to decide on an appropriate timescale and seeking expert advice may help mould your monitoring plan.

Overleaf is an example of a *wheel of success* following the first monitoring cycle. You can clearly see where progress has been made and the size of the change from the initial profile. Importantly, you can also identify those areas where no progress has been made. This may be expected if you planned not to make any progress in a specific determinant of success in a single monitoring cycle. However, failure to progress in a determinant to which you have dedicated time, effort and resource should raise concern and result in a close examination of your prescription. While it is uncommon, if you move backwards in any determinants you've made a significant error in prescription that needs to be addressed in the next cycle.

Having monitored your progress you are now in a position to adapt your prescription in line with observed changes for your next phase.

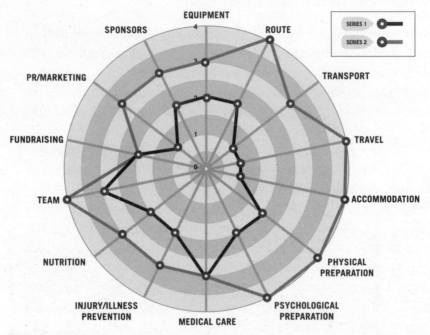

Monitoring how far you have progressed in each determinant of success gives instant visual feedback on the efficacy of your prescription and provides a platform to tailor your next phase of prescription to optimize progression.

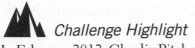 *Challenge Highlight*

In February 2012, Charlie Pitcher broke the solo transatlantic rowing record, making the crossing in just over thirty days. This incredible achievement was made all the more amazing by the fact that when Charlie first came to see me, he had never rowed before.

One of our primary targets on Charlie's *wheel of success* was his physical performance – a critical determinant in an event that relies entirely on one individual to succeed. Following an initial profile against the 'gold standard' requirements, I prescribed a bespoke programme for each physiological determinant of success which progressed from rowing ergometer to on-water. Detailed monitoring of Charlie's progress at six-week intervals allowed me to mould the programme to optimize his physiological performance. Alongside this preparation we built in a variety of other determinants including

Record breaker. Meticulous monitoring of physiological performance provided critical information in the prescription of training.

psychological, nutritional and technical. Targeting each determinant of success, Charlie progressively moved his *wheel of success* to the outer rim of excellence. With excellence in all determinants of success in place, Charlie delivered his vision of becoming the fastest man to row the Atlantic.

▲▲ *www.achievetheimpossible.co.uk*

IT'S ALL IN THE DETAIL

Having clearly defined your determinants of success, the next step is to establish a detailed understanding of each determinant. Taking a reductionist view of each determinant by dissecting them into their component parts will allow you to better understand what is required to deliver success in each determinant and will also provide a platform to Profile-Prescribe-Monitor. The detail required for this task often relies on expert advice in each determinant. The more time and effort you put into this process the more effective your prescription will be and the greater your chance of optimizing your *wheel of success*. A common mistake is to brush over this critical element in the planning process and hope for the best!

Below is an example of how to dissect the physical preparation determinant of success for an ultra-endurance running challenge into its component parts and create a *wheel of success*. Please bear with me while I put my scientific hat on again! While the example is specific to an endurance running challenge, the concept of dissecting each determinant into its component parts is applicable to and important for all challenges.

The first step is to identify the determinants of success for running performance which include the following: maximum aerobic capacity ($\dot{V}O_{2max}$), running velocity at $\dot{V}O_{2max}$ ($v\dot{V}O_{2max}$), maximum running velocity ($\dot{V}_{max}$), running economy and lactate threshold (LT). Opposite is a schematic of the component parts of running

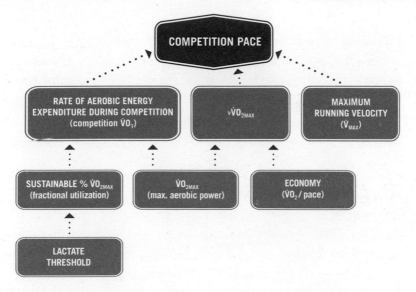

Physiological determinants of competition pace in endurance running performance.

performance demonstrating the type of detail required to move closer to optimizing your *delivery of success*.

Having established your determinants of success for your 'physical performance' determinant you can create your *wheel of success* (see overleaf) and enter your Profile-Prescribe-Monitor cycle as detailed earlier. You can use different scoring systems when examining the component elements of each overall determinant of success. The key is to choose a system which best represents your ability to monitor change and which you understand.

For example, when examining the physiological determinants of success I like to use a percentage of the 'gold standard' scoring system as it allows small changes in performance to be monitored and recognized. In this way, rather than requiring a 25% improvement in performance before making an observable change to the *wheel of success*, I am able to demonstrate changes as small as 1%, which is more valuable when monitoring the impact of prescription.

Overleaf is an example of an initial profile and the results of the first monitoring phase for the physiological determinants of our

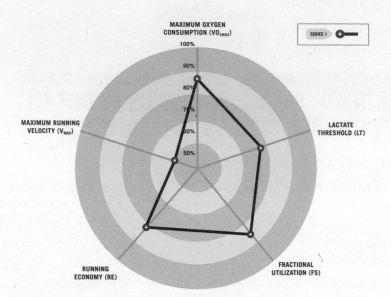

Wheel of success showing the physiological determinants of running performance for a runner profiled against the 100% 'gold standard'.

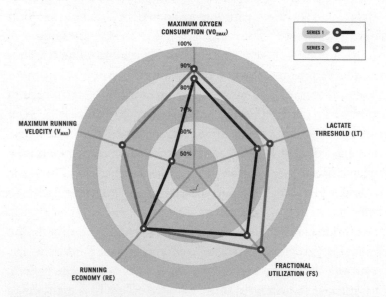

Wheel of success showing the changes to the physiological determinants of running performance following the initial prescription and monitoring phase.

runner. You will see that the centre of the *wheel of success* starts at 50%, which allows for better visualization of small changes.

IDENTIFYING THE RISKS AND ENSURING THAT ALL POTENTIAL OUTCOMES ARE ACCOUNTED FOR

A common mistake is to concentrate all your efforts on the determinants of success without recognizing the importance of those factors that could, at best, result in a reduction in performance or, at worst, lead to the end of a challenge. While it is rarely possible to eliminate risk, the purpose of risk management is to limit its potential impact on performance. Identifying risks is not in itself enough, you must develop solutions for every eventuality in order to ensure you limit their negative impact on performance.

If you have no prior experience of challenges or you are taking on a new challenge for the first time it can be difficult to identify potential risks to success. Seeking expert advice and talking to others who have experience of the challenge you are planning can be incredibly valuable. Spending a little time researching the risks can be the difference between success and failure.

There are common mistakes that people make on a regular basis that can have a devastating impact on performance. A great example of this is using new, untested equipment for the challenge. You only have to watch the London Marathon to see runners who have decided to use a new pair of trainers for the event. The result is often clear to see, with blood seeping through having given an unwanted red tinge to the sparkling new shoes.

A simple internet search can identify most of the common risks to success and often provide generic solutions. While this is a good start to risk management, the next step is to tailor the generic risks to your own situation and identify those risks that are specific to your performance. This may not be quite so easy in the absence of experience; however, this is one of the primary roles of the preparation process, which we will examine in detail in Chapter 5 – The Road to Success.

BESPOKE TAILORING

Preparation is not solely about the physical determinants; it should also be used as a tool to identify solutions to risks that may hinder performance. For example, nutrition is a key element of any challenge, and it is almost entirely individual. Generic advice is available, but you will need to design your own nutrition strategy to reduce the risk of low energy levels, dehydration, etc. The best way to develop solutions is through trial and error in the preparation phase. It doesn't matter if you get it wrong during preparation: failure is positive at that point if you learn from your mistakes and develop an alternative strategy that works. A common mistake is to adopt a generic strategy because it has worked for others or is recommended as part of general guidance. Remember, individually tailored solutions are far more likely to reduce risks to your performance.

Never assume a risk is too small to worry about. Equally, never assume that you cannot address risks you have no control over. For example, you cannot control the weather, but what you can do is ensure you have taken account of the potential impact of likely weather and identified solutions to limit the potential impact of adverse conditions (i.e. the right equipment).

A common misconception is that focusing on risks is a negative process which has the potential to create self-doubt and loss of confidence. However, if managed appropriately, the identification of solutions to potential risks can be incredibly empowering and lead to enhanced self-confidence. There are a number of ways to tackle the issue of risk and solution, but my personal approach is to use 'If–Then' plans which can be constructed for each of the determinants of success.

THE 'IF–THEN' PLAN

'If–Then' plans can be really helpful in dealing with potential risks. 'If–Then' plans work by putting the risk to performance alongside the solution. By putting risks and solutions side by side, the process of implementing the solution can become automated. During the preparation for a major challenge, practising the 'If–Then' plan can minimize the risk and also enhance your confidence: you know you can deal with the risk. 'If–Then' plans can restructure negative thoughts about the risks to success and turn them into positive thoughts, simply by having a pre-prepared structured solution.

In a challenge which requires a team of specialists, it is important that the entire team understands the 'If–Then' plan so that they can ensure its optimal execution. Once you have constructed your 'If–Then' plans, collate them into a single resource and ensure that you share them with the entire team so that everyone knows what to do. Below is an example 'If–Then' plan for equipment failure on a cycle challenge.

If (risk to performance)	Then (solution to the risk)
If I get a puncture on the road when I am alone	**Then** I remind myself of times when I have changed a tube, keep calm, change the inner tube and inform the team at the next stop that I have used my spare tube and gas refill
If my chain breaks	**Then** I say to myself 'Problems happen' and focus on what to do; I do not start catastrophizing. I will call my support team to let them know my chain has broken and that I am attempting to fix it myself. I will ask the team to start heading towards my location and I will call them once I have fixed the chain

If my lights are running low on battery	**Then** I will use my spare light which I am carrying with me and inform the team at the next stop
If my wheel is buckled	**Then** I will say to myself 'Problems happen' and focus on what to do; I do not start catastrophizing. I will call my support team to meet me at my location to change the wheel
If my gears are not changing smoothly or are jumping	**Then** I will inform my support team at the next stop and have them repaired
If I have a catastrophic failure of my bike	**Then** I will call my support team to tell them what has happened and where to meet me. I will then put my jacket on and find shelter until the team arrive

Having established your vision and identified your SMART goals along your *road to success*, the next phase in your journey was to establish the determinants of success. Armed with the determinants of success you were able to construct a *wheel of success* and through a continuous process of Profile-Prescribe-Monitor identify your strengths and weaknesses and take a targeted approach to moving each determinant to create a wheel of excellence. In order to optimize the *delivery of success* you must then identify the risks to performance and create solutions using an 'If–Then' plan like the one above. With these in place you are ready to begin the planning and preparation for your challenge.

Challenge Highlight

In 2012, comedian John Bishop undertook a five-day ultra-endurance challenge for Sport Relief. The challenge required John to cycle 186 miles from Paris to Calais on day 1; then on day 2 row across the Channel with the support of three fellow celebrities; and finally run 86 miles over three days from Dover to London.

As you can imagine, there are a large number of determinants of success to consider for a challenge of this magnitude. Furthermore, the risks to such an iconic challenge are significant and somewhat unique. Although the Sport Relief challenges are one-offs because of the very high national profile linked to significant media coverage and a BBC documentary, combined with the incredible sums of money raised (John raised £4.5 million), the approach to delivering success is no different to the same challenge on a much less public stage (with the exception of the size of the team, which in this case included in excess of eighty people from a range of areas including: a film crew; a Threshold Sports logistics team; a Comic Relief fund-raising and PR team).

Having defined the challenge, I worked closely with the team to establish the determinants of success and create a *wheel of success*. We then entered the Profile-Prescribe-Monitor cycle over three months to ensure optimal preparation of John and the team for the challenge. The risks to a challenge of this magnitude created a significant 'If–Then' plan, which was acted upon on a regular basis. The most obvious use of the 'If–Then' plan was during the rowing element. As we will discuss in Chapter 5 – The Road to Success, it is not unusual to have to adapt the plan during the challenge to ensure success. Any changes made should usually have been pre-empted in the 'If–Then' plan, which was true for the rowing element on day 2 of John's challenge.

On day 1 John cycled the 186 miles from Paris to Calais, but because of the weather (heavy rain and headwinds) the ride took longer than predicted, finishing at 4.30 a.m. After only two hours' sleep, John had to board the boat along with his team-mates Davina McCall, Freddie Flintoff and Denise Lewis for the rowing leg. We couldn't change the launch time because it was fixed by the tides – you can't change nature!

The potential sleep deprivation had been planned for in the 'If–Then' plan. As the team reached the halfway point, four hours into the row, John began to fade badly, which raised significant concerns from the team. With the 'solution' to the 'risk' of sleep deprivation in place, we acted to minimize the impact by giving John high-dose caffeine to combat the psychological fatigue, combined with a high-energy supplement to stave off physical fatigue. Knowing the speed at which both supplements enter the system (around thirty minutes), John and the team were instructed to set

John Bishop's 'Week of Hell'. A training run tailored specifically to optimize the determinants of success and reduce the risks associated with the 86-mile run over three days from Dover to London.

off rowing at a very light pace and begin to increase effort gradually, in line with the impact of the supplements. Within half an hour the team were back to full speed and continued on to a successful arrival in Dover, demonstrating the value of an 'If–Then' plan executed rapidly.

▲▲ *www.achievetheimpossible.co.uk*

TASK
- Using the SMART principles you have read and understood from Chapter 2, construct a set of short-, medium- and long-term goals.
- Having established your vision and passed it through your Flow of Success, identify the determinants of success and construct a time plan leading up to the challenge.
- Create a *wheel of success* and profile yourself against your determinants of success using a simple scale to track your progress.
- Take each individual determinant and identify the component parts.
- Create a *wheel of success* and profile yourself against each component using a simple scale to track your progress.
- Monitor yourself at regular intervals to identify your progress.
  - Pick a timescale for monitoring that works for you but give yourself time to deliver changes.
- Identify the risks to performance and construct an 'If–Then' plan to deal with every risk.

CHAPTER FOUR

THE BRAIN OF SUCCESS

Belief, commitment and motivation

Identifying your vision and establishing its importance is not enough to ensure the *delivery of success*. We have established that hard work is the foundation upon which your *road to success* is built. However, in order to ensure you continue to work hard during the steep ascents of your Mountain of Success, you will need support from your *brain of success*.

Of the four limits to success (Body, Mind, Technical, Environment) it is the brain that has the greatest potential to form barriers to success on a continual basis. Developing the *brain of success* is not solely about nature, it is also about nurture. There is no doubt that some people are born with the architecture required to support a *brain of success*, evidenced by a history of successful challenges. But we all have the ability to build and develop our own *brain of success* around the three key building blocks of belief, commitment and motivation.

Belief, commitment and motivation are intimately linked. The rise or fall of one element will have a direct impact on the other two elements. For example, commitment can change throughout a challenge due to a rise or dip in belief and motivation. As your motivation falls you tend to question whether you are able to achieve success and as a result reduce your commitment to the challenge. In contrast, if your belief in your ability to deliver success rises you will be more motivated and committed to delivering success.

This variation in belief, commitment and motivation throughout a challenge is natural and should be expected. The key to delivering success is ensuring that none of the three elements is reduced to a critically low level. Losing belief, commitment or motivation completely can be catastrophic to the success of a challenge and you should regularly check your levels. Taking ownership of your challenge will lead to the optimal development of your *brain of success* and deliver success.

By the end of this chapter you will have gained an understanding of:

- The three fundamental elements of the *brain of success*:
  - Commitment
  - Belief
  - Motivation
- The 'dark times'
- The Balance of Motivation
  - The 'need to achieve' versus the 'fear of failure'
- How to overcome the fear of failure
- Incentives to success
- Contracts of success
- The redundancy model
- David Walliams's big swim (challenge highlight)

THE CONTRACT OF COMMITMENT

Success cannot be delivered without commitment. Commitment is not simply saying that you will dedicate the hard work, time and resources required for the challenge. Words are cheap and commitment is worthless unless you have a clear understanding of the challenge, the limits to achieving success and the determinants of success. Only then will you be able to make a realistic, well-informed commitment to the challenge. A commitment can be viewed as a promise to deliver on your vision. By making a pledge to commit the

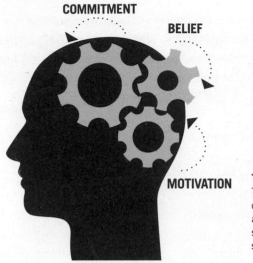

COMMITMENT

BELIEF

MOTIVATION

The *brain of success.*
The interlinked elements
of belief, commitment
and motivation turning
simultaneously to deliver
success.

required effort, time and resources you are creating a contract with yourself and others stating that you will do everything in your control to deliver success. Commitment is fundamental from the very start of your challenge, and while it may vary in intensity throughout the challenge, related to your changing belief and motivation, it is crucial that you remain committed.

BELIEF WAS NOT BUILT IN A DAY

You are very unlikely to enter a challenge with the absolute belief that you will be successful. This is only natural, and rather than creating negative thinking it should provide positive reinforcement that your vision is worth achieving: if success was a foregone conclusion it wouldn't be worth achieving! Unlike motivation, which is often at its peak at the start of a challenge, belief builds progressively throughout your challenge. By optimizing planning and preparation and targeting your determinants of success, you will continually provide

85

positive feedback about your ability to deliver success which will lead to a constantly increasing belief. Challenging yourself regularly with your short- and medium-term goals provides objective feedback on your ability, resulting in increased confidence throughout the preparation phase. Belief grows with a greater certainty of success.

NOT EVERYTHING THAT SHINES IS GOLD

Success is a valuable commodity that should never be taken for granted. The failure of many challenges often occurs because of complacency associated with a belief that success is easily attainable and does not require commitment. This loss of commitment rapidly leads to a loss of motivation and catastrophic failure of the challenge as the early positive results are not replicated.

One of the main reasons why only 10% of dieters keep their weight off in the long term is because of complacency linked to rapid weight loss in the first six weeks. This early success leads to the belief that reductions in weight will continue at the same rate without commitment. Sadly, this is not the case, and as the brakes are applied to the weight-loss journey, motivation falls until the challenge is, once again, assigned to the workshop awaiting repairs before the next diet journey begins.

We often regard this response as 'over-confidence', which usually spells disaster for a challenge. There is no doubt that belief in your ability to deliver success is crucial; however, you must be careful to maintain respect for the challenge. Keep in mind the law of diminishing returns and the fact that you will have to maintain your commitment to the challenge and continue to work hard if you are to be successful.

NATURE VERSUS NURTURE

Motivation describes the force within us which leads us to behave in a certain way (motivation is derived from the Latin *movere*, meaning 'to move'). There are numerous terms which are used to describe this force, including 'drive', 'guts' and 'inspiration'. Whatever term we use, there is no doubt that motivation is important when it comes to delivering success and that successful people are highly motivated.

What is also true is that some people have a greater intrinsic motivation and these highly motivated people have a great deal of belief in their own ability. We all have friends who are always taking on new challenges, searching for success in every aspect of their lives. To that end, there is some truth in the fact that highly motivated people are born; however, it is also true that motivation can be developed. We all have some degree of motivation. The key is in understanding how we can maximize and maintain our reserves of motivation to ensure we maintain belief in and commitment to our challenge.

THE MOTIVATION ROLLER-COASTER

Imagine your motivation is like the fuel in your car as you travel along your *road to success*. As you start your journey your long-term goal (your vision) fills your fuel tank with motivation. Often you find your fuel tank overflowing with motivation which must be controlled if you are to use your precious energy source efficiently.

As you travel along your *road to success* you will begin to use up your fuel, which leads to a reduction in motivation. This is entirely normal and of no concern – unless you allow your fuel gauge to move into the 'red zone'. At this point you stand a chance of losing all motivation, which would be disastrous for your challenge. Short- and medium-term goals provide the regular service-station stops which allow you to continually top up your motivation. For this reason, motivation varies constantly throughout a challenge. You cannot remain fully motivated throughout, and accepting periods of reduced motivation will allow you to maintain your belief in delivering success.

Meticulous planning will significantly reduce the chances of major reductions in motivation. It is rare for any challenge not to have 'dark times'. These periods result in you seriously questioning your ability to deliver success and put your belief in jeopardy. In my experience these episodes are unavoidable and, like potholes, they are often difficult to predict. 'Dark times' are dangerous if they are not handled appropriately.

EVERY CLOUD HAS A SILVER LINING

'Dark times', then, are almost inevitable in challenges that push us to the boundaries of our capabilities. Accepting that they may occur is the first step in dealing with these potentially challenge-ending episodes. 'Dark times' are enormous barriers that rise up rapidly and without warning. What makes them so challenging is their multi-faceted nature. They tend to be associated with multiple limits of performance, which makes them difficult to deal with.

 Challenge Highlight

In 2011, I trained David Walliams to swim the length of the Thames (140 miles in eight days) for Sport Relief. Following a particularly difficult second day consisting of fourteen hours of non-stop swimming, David got just four hours of sleep, which was constantly interrupted by vomiting and diarrhoea. When I woke David at 4.30 a.m. on day 3 ahead of a 5.30 a.m. start, the combination of sleep deprivation, dehydration, fatigue and illness marked a significant 'dark time' which had moved his motivation into the 'red zone'.

However, like barriers, the component parts that give rise to the 'dark times' can be planned for ahead of time. Armed with the

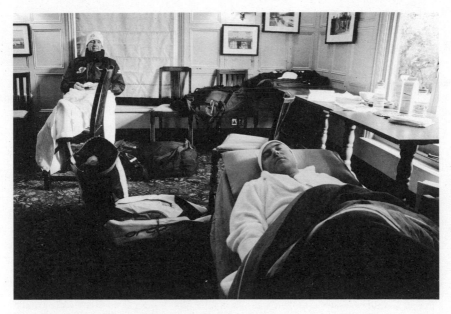

'Dark times'. Day 3 on the 'Walliams versus The Thames' challenge, and David is experiencing one of the toughest episodes of the challenge.

solution to each limit of success, the 'dark times' can be overcome. In the case of Walliams versus The Thames we tackled the sickness with a combination of azithromycin (an antibiotic) and an anti-emetic (anti-sickness); the dehydration and low energy with a combination of an electrolyte and carbohydrate fluid; and fatigue with a change to the short-term performance goals for day 3: David would swim eighteen miles rather than twenty-two. Making the goal for day 3 feel easier helped bridge the gap between how much energy David felt he had and how much energy he felt he needed for the task. When you set yourself a difficult goal, it can feel overwhelming, and the uncertainty this brings is often accompanied by a feeling of tiredness. The meticulous planning combined with the use of established 'If–Then' scenarios allowed David to go on to complete day 3 and subsequently conquer the Thames.

www.achievetheimpossible.co.uk

THE TRIPLE TARGET

From your *wheel of success* you will be able to identify those determinants of success which provide greatest intrinsic motivation. These determinants are usually strengths and those which you enjoy the most. For example, if your goal is weight management and you find reducing calorie consumption much easier than being more active, you will focus your attention on diet and let your exercise programme fall by the wayside. This variation in intrinsic motivation is important as your motivation for a determinant will affect three key factors:

1. Selection: Which determinants you select to tackle and in which order is driven by how motivated you are. Focusing on the determinants of success that are strengths or are enjoyable will provide a high level of motivation, so it is likely you will select these above weak determinants. However, when you get good at the determinants you like, remember the determinants you do not like doing so much.
2. Persistence: The high levels of motivation linked to your strengths mean you will persevere much more towards delivering excellence compared with weak determinants.
3. Intensity: High motivation leads to a high work rate to deliver success. In contrast, the low motivation linked to weak determinants leads to poor commitment to working hard.

This is a very natural approach to take as you place a great deal of importance and are successful in the determinants in which you are strong and/or find enjoyable. In other words, strong determinants possess a high 'need to achieve' combined with a low 'fear of failure' which results in high levels of motivation.

While performance will improve with this approach, it is the enhancement of your weaknesses that are likely to reap the greatest rewards. Unfortunately, it is these areas that create the lowest levels of motivation as they are linked to a low 'need to achieve' and a high 'fear of failure'. As a result, having selected them you are likely to be less persistent and take on a lower work rate to achieve success. To deliver success you will need to ensure you optimize your motivation for all determinants of success.

THE BALANCE OF MOTIVATION

There are two key factors which affect motivation during a major challenge: the need to achieve and the fear of failure. The need to achieve describes our desire to be successful, and fear of failure refers to the way in which we view the possibility of defeat. These two factors are independent personality characteristics and as such you may possess high levels of both or lower levels of one compared with the other. The balance of the need to achieve and fear of failure will ultimately dictate your ability to deliver success. Use the Balance of Motivation (overleaf) to identify what category of performer you currently fit into: 'The Achiever', 'The Indifferent' or 'The Failure'.

ALL IS NOT LOST

By understanding yourself and establishing your levels of need to achieve and fear of failure you will gain a greater understanding of what is required to enhance your motivation. While motivation is in part associated with what you were born with, we know that it can be consciously manipulated and therefore, by redressing the balance between your need to achieve and fear of failure, you can make the changes necessary to deliver success.

Imagine your need to achieve is your accelerator pedal and

THE ACHIEVER: *You are a person that loves a challenge. You are highly motivated and committed to delivering success. You love to win but realize that failure is only present when you fail to learn.*

* This is your target balance.

THE INDIFFERENT: *You are a person that needs to be challenged and are often highly motivated at the start of a challenge; however, failure lowers your belief which reduces your commitment to the challenge. This balance in 'need to achieve' and 'fear of failure' often results in very low motivation and a person that sees little benefit in a challenge.*

* You must change the balance of motivation in favour of your need to achieve by reducing your fear of failure and increasing your need to achieve.

THE FAILURE: *You are a person that avoids a challenge unless you know you are certain to win. You are poorly motivated in the face of a challenge as you are certain you will fail. Your low levels of belief result in you losing commitment rapidly, often leaving jobs unfinished.*

*This is a catastrophic position to start any challenge. You must work hard to address the balance before committing to a major challenge.

The Balance of Motivation. The relationship between your 'need to achieve' and your 'fear of failure' will ultimately dictate your ability to deliver success.

your fear of failure is your brake pedal. How much pressure you apply to each pedal will dictate how fast you travel. Too much pressure on the brake or too little pressure on the accelerator and your journey will come to a premature end. Your focus should be on shifting the balance to achieve additional pressure on the accelerator and reduced pressure on the brake. With this analogy in mind, imagine the pressure you apply is graded on a 0 to 5 scale; identify where you would rank the pressure you currently apply to each pedal.

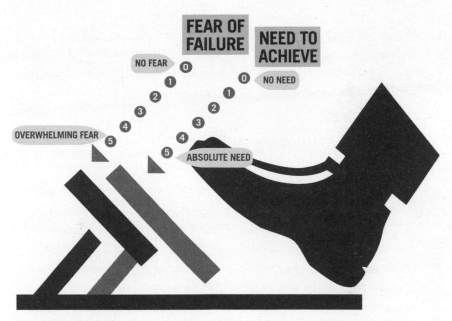

The Pedals of Motivation. Rank your 'fear of failure' and 'need to achieve' to establish the speed of your journey. Then target strategies to increase your need to achieve and reduce your fear of failure to deliver success.

DISPELLING THE FEAR

Fear of failure is often driven by an unrealistic long-term goal (your vision) or poorly constructed short- and medium-term goals. Remember the SMART approach to goal setting. By making your goals more realistic and achievable you will reduce your fear of failure. In addition, by repeatedly achieving success through your short-term goals you will begin to reduce the fear of failure and move towards becoming an 'Achiever'.

For example, if your goal is to run the London Marathon and you have never run before, the fear of failure is likely to far outweigh your need to achieve. If, however, you set your short- and medium-term goals to run 5km, then 10km, then 10 miles, and finally a half marathon prior to reaching your long-term goal of the marathon, you will have significantly reduced your fear of failure. Positive affirmation in this way increases your motivation, your belief and, as a result, your commitment to delivering success.

CONTROL YOUR OWN DESTINY

Fear of failure is also associated with a concern that the outcome is outside your control. The key to reducing your fear of failure is to take control. Believing that failure is inevitable and something that you can do nothing about will result in low motivation and commitment. You must gain ownership of the challenge to fully develop your *brain of success*. Gaining ownership of the challenge will always result in an increased motivation to work hard to deliver success. For example, if your challenge is to lose weight it is always more motivating to take responsibility rather than leave it to others to lead the challenge. This approach does not mean you work alone. You continue to work with your specialist team (nutrition, physical activity, etc.) but now you are the leader rather than a follower. Taking control will maintain your commitment to the challenge as you have tailored all aspects of planning and preparation to your own journey along your *road to success*.

DON'T BLAME ME!

Having established ownership you are now fully accountable for the outcome of your challenge. In other words, *you* are ultimately responsible for delivering success. This can be a very scary but an incredibly important step to take. By taking responsibility you only have one person to blame if things go wrong. For this reason many people stop short of taking full ownership to give them the luxury of blaming others. This is counterproductive as it leads to a lack of commitment which in turn reduces motivation and will ultimately limit success.

I always like to use the analogy of money to articulate this point. Imagine you are buying a car; would you work hard over a long period of time to earn the money and then give the responsibility of buying the car to someone who will never drive it after they have purchased it? With that in mind, why would you allow someone else to control the planning, preparation and delivery of your vision? Rather than viewing responsibility as negative, see it as empowering: you have now become the master of your own destiny, able to control the planning and preparation for your challenge, overcome hurdles and make rapid, informed decisions to negotiate potholes along your *road to success*.

THE CENTRAL MOTIVATOR

The motivation for a long-term goal is often anchored around a single factor. The achievement of success may bring rewards in a variety of ways, but there will be one motivator that transcends all others and acts as the primary driving force behind success. The central motivator is a powerful incentive that generally tends to be linked to an intrinsic reward that is very important to you or has the ability to move you or others out of an environment that causes suffering. The central motivator has a key role to play in overcoming barriers and dealing with potholes. It is 'dark times' in particular that seriously challenge our belief, and in my experience it is at these times that the central motivator becomes the most potent stimulus to commitment. Reminding yourself why you are taking on the challenge can tip the balance in favour of continuing towards your long-term goal and success.

INCENTIVES TO SUCCESS

Many of us will take on major challenges to raise money for charity to help those less fortunate than ourselves. Every year hundreds of thousands of people run marathons around the world to raise billions of pounds for charity. With the exception of the elite runners, there is no palpable reward for this endeavour other than our own shared pride in achieving something very special.

In my experience, these intrinsic rewards are far more powerful than physical rewards. For example, promising yourself a new car or a holiday if you are successful rarely provides sustained, long-term motivation, as the likelihood is you have the means to award yourself these prizes without reaching your long-term goal. For example, if you are aiming to lose weight, rather than reward yourself with a slap-up meal, focus on getting into that dress you haven't worn for ten years. When you put on the dress for the first time and go out in public the sense of achievement will be overwhelming and more powerful than any Michelin-starred menu.

Of course, the major reward at the end of your challenge is unlikely to provide sufficient motivation to fuel your entire journey along the *road to success*. I tend to use two strategies to maintain motivation: token rewards and personal contracts.

THE SPOILS OF WAR

There are a number of different strategies to help enhance your motivation. It is important to remember that there is unlikely to be one single strategy that works for you. You should be prepared to try different strategies until you find the one which works best. Whatever your strategy, there is one truth: you must celebrate success.

We all recognize the importance of celebrating when we reach our long-term goal. However, it is important to remember

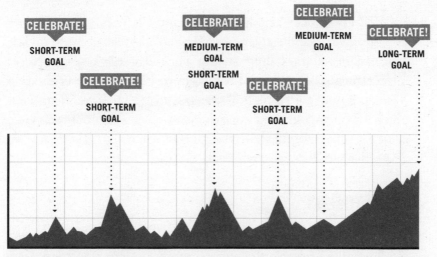

The mountain-top celebrations. Celebrating the successful delivery of your goals along your *road to success* is crucial in maintaining your motivation and commitment to your challenge.

that reaching the milestone of a short- or medium-term goal is an achievement in itself and should be rewarded accordingly. My approach is to use rewards on a continual basis; but the size of the reward should be linked to the size of the goal, so bigger rewards for medium-term goals compared with short-term goals. Celebrating success is important as you will fill up your tank of motivation as it becomes clear that your effort is being rewarded.

TOKENS OF SUCCESS

Token rewards are small prizes that symbolize achievement. They have little or no value but can carry great prestige as indicators of achievement. For example, an Olympic gold medal has little monetary value but it is a powerful sign of success. You are unlikely to be aiming for Olympic glory, but the same reward system holds true for any challenge. The value of the reward is much less important than the esteem in which it is held.

Token rewards come in various forms including the awarding of a trophy or a certificate; an email or social media post to update progress; or simply telling people of your achievements. Never underestimate the power of recognition. Placing your goals on a chart in a public area such as on your fridge at home or on your office wall, and ticking off the successful achievement of each goal, can be a very powerful motivational tool when your family, friends and colleagues comment positively on your progress.

TEAM TOKENS

If you are taking on a challenge as part of a team you could adapt a system of token rewards to enhance motivation. As a modern pent-athlete I used to train for over thirty-five hours a week. Motivation was often in short supply, particularly in the deep-winter phases of training. As a result we developed weekly competitions that were of inconsequential monetary value but hugely important to those involved. My favourite example was 'The Ice Cream Shoot-Off'. The ultimate aim of the competition was to shoot to the very best of our abilities but the reward for winning was an ice cream paid for by the rest of the team. Far more important than the cost of the ice cream was the kudos attached to winning, which created a potent stimulus to motivation.

This example demonstrates the value of token rewards among a team of performers focused on delivering the same outcome, but you could equally use this approach across your entire team, despite them working on different elements of a challenge.

In order to ensure the team-token strategy enhances motivation you should follow the **SCORE** approach:

Simplicity: Avoid complexity. Make sure everyone understands how they can achieve success.
Consistency: As the leader you can take responsibility of awarding

the reward or appoint an official adjudicator. Either way the
reward should be seen to be fairly awarded.

Observation: Every member of the team should feel they are
included and have the same chance of success.

Reward: Remember, it is the perceived value of the reward that is
more important than its monetary value. Work at raising the
kudos and public recognition of the award.

Explanation: Explain what is required to win the reward and ensure
that everyone understands what they have to achieve to be
successful.

CONTRACTS OF SUCCESS

Making a contract with yourself to deliver an outcome is particularly
valuable when your motivation is low. This is often the case with
determinants that are low in importance in one or more of the trio
of motivation: Selection, Persistence and Intensity. By formalizing
an arrangement detailing your goal and when you will deliver it, you
are much more likely to be successful.

This may seem a slightly bizarre approach but the more formal
the contract, the greater the chances of delivering on your commitment to it. Your contract raises the selective importance of your goal
and provides the necessary motivation to persist with the appropriate
amount of work until you have delivered success. By asking a third
party, someone close to you, to witness the contract you will raise the
importance of the contract and the level of responsibility on you to
deliver. As with rewards, placing the contract in a public place will
also increase the importance of your commitment to the contract
and raise the profile of the reward once you deliver success. Here
are some examples of personal contracts you could adapt for your
own challenge.

Personal Contract 1 (weight management and alcohol consumption)

I, the undersigned, do hereby promise that I will not drink alcohol on a weekday evening and I will limit my consumption to 12 units of alcohol at the weekends.

Name:_____

Signed:_____

Witnessed:_____

Personal Contract 2 (major challenge and travel confirmation)

I, the undersigned, promise to make all arrangements pertaining to the travel of all team members to the major challenge by the final day of September. I will contact all team members with details of travel arrangements within a week of making the final bookings.

Name:_____

Signed:_____

Witnessed:_____

Personal Contract 3 (business and family life balance)

I, the undersigned, do hereby promise that I will not respond to any emails after seven p.m. on a weekday and will allocate a single hour (six p.m. to seven p.m.) to answering important emails on the weekend.

Name:_____

Signed:_____

Witnessed (Wife/Husband):_____

IT'S THE WAY YOU ACT

How you see yourself is fundamentally important to your commitment, belief and motivation. By believing you can achieve success and constantly reaffirming that belief through achievement of your goals, you will create a confidence that permeates into those around you. If you believe, your family, friends and colleagues will believe in you. How others see you and your challenge is important in developing your *brain of success*. If they believe you can do it, they will provide motivation and support your commitment. By acting like a winner you are much more likely to achieve long-term success even in the event of short-term failure. Remember, failure is not failure if you learn something and use that knowledge to adapt your approach to bring about future success. Having a positive outlook on failing to reach a short-term goal will empower you, creating the motivation to address the shortcomings in your approach and ensure the successful delivery of your goal in the future.

THE REDUNDANCY MODEL

My approach to the *brain of success* is one of 'redundancy'. My primary goal is one of metamorphosis: to move the stimulus for developing the *brain of success* from extrinsic (provided by sources outside of self) to intrinsic (sourced within self). You must be fully committed; You must have self-belief; and You must be self-motivated.

This does not mean the removal of extrinsic contributions. Extrinsic motivation provides support particularly during difficult times when motivation may be in short supply. Positive reinforcement throughout the preparation phase supports the *brain of success*.

Challenge Highlight

In August 2005, I received a phone call from the CEO of Comic Relief, Kevin Cahill. What followed was an extraordinary request: 'David Walliams has suggested he would be prepared to attempt to swim the English Channel for Sport Relief. Can you train him?'

The request was astonishing on a number of levels. First, the Channel is the 'blue riband' of open-water swimming challenges. As we saw with the challenge highlight in Chapter 1 – The Scales of Success, it is regarded as the toughest open-water swim on the planet. More people have summited Everest than have successfully swum the Channel. Second, David Walliams was at best an ordinary swimmer. Third, nothing like this had ever been attempted before by such a high-profile celebrity. The challenge was certainly audacious. Given my belief that you should grasp opportunities when they present themselves, I agreed to meet David and discuss the project.

As with all the major challenges I have been part of, the primary purpose of my first meeting was to establish whether David possessed the ability to develop a *brain of success*. This process cannot be achieved in a single session, as we have seen; however, there is always great value to looking into someone's eyes when you are establishing their commitment to a major challenge. While belief grows throughout the preparation process, commitment is absolutely fundamental from the very beginning. Having described, in detail, the reality of what would be required to deliver success in this challenge, and despite the fact he had no experience whatsoever of open-water swimming, it was clear that David was fully committed.

David's motivation was apparent from the very beginning. The initial conversation between David and Kevin regarding the challenge had taken place on returning from Ethiopia where they had been visiting Comic Relief projects. One project in particular became the central motivator for the entire challenge. During a visit to a shelter for young girls who had been systematically abused, David was so moved that he truly believed he could and should do something important to raise awareness and funds for the life-changing work of Comic Relief.

We spoke only occasionally about this central motivator, reserving its power for those very 'dark times' – those critical moments which define the outcome of a challenge. I remember distinctly one such moment prior to the start of the swim. On board the boat travelling to the start point of Shakespeare Beach,

Comic Relief hardman and legend: David Walliams has completed three ultra-endurance swims and an ultra-endurance cycle. Though the central motivator and his motivation changed with each challenge, one aspect remained constant: success.

and in a moment of quiet reflection, I reminded David why he had embarked on the challenge. David's ability to change the lives of those young girls in Ethiopia, to move them out of an environment that causes suffering, was a potent reminder of his commitment to the challenge, and despite thirty-three weeks of gruelling training, he started his challenge with optimal motivation. Ten hours and thirty-five minutes after leaving Shakespeare Beach, David reached Cap Gris-Nez and in doing so became the first person ever to raise £1 million in a solo, one-off challenge.

www.achievetheimpossible.co.uk

TASK
- Write down your motivation (why you are taking on the challenge).
- Write down the rewards you are going to use along your *road to success* to ensure you stay motivated.
- Identify what category of performer you currently are on the Balance of Motivation.
- Estimate your own level of 'need to achieve' and 'fear of failure'.
- Establish what you are going to do about increasing your need to achieve and reducing your fear of failure.
- Draw your Mountain of Success and identify what rewards you will award each short- and medium-term goal.
- Write a draft personal contract that you can use should the need arise.

CHAPTER FIVE

THE ROAD TO SUCCESS

Detailed planning and preparation for optimal performance

We all know that we have to prepare for a major challenge; but preparation is not an ad hoc series of events that culminate magically in success. Planning the preparation phase for any challenge is crucial if you are to move every determinant of success as close as possible to the outer circle of excellence in your *wheel of success* with the resources you have available. Your plan should be constructed using macro-, meso- and micro-cycles along a timeline that aligns to the signposts of the short-, medium- and long-term goals along your *road to success*. Once you have created a detailed plan of your journey you are in a position to start the preparation for your challenge. Establishing an intelligent working approach to your preparation using the key principles of preparation will allow you to target your determinants of success and optimize your chances of success.

By the end of this chapter you will have gained an understanding of:

- How to construct a plan based on your long-, medium- and short-term goals
- How to structure your *road to success* using macro-, meso- and micro-cycles
- Jon Smith's North Pole Marathon in 2011 (challenge highlight)
- How to prepare for your challenge using the principles of preparation
- How to optimize your preparation and avoid common mistakes
- Davina McCall's ultra-endurance triathlon (challenge highlight)

FAILING TO PLAN IS PLANNING TO FAIL

A plan is not simply a sequential list of tasks. It should be a detailed map of what, why, when and how you are going to deliver your short-, medium- and, ultimately, long-term goals. The start of the planning process is establishing your goals. Your short-, medium- and long-term goals provide the signposts which will act as your guide when constructing your *road to success*. Much like the short-, medium- and long-term goal setting discussed in Chapter 2 – The Vision of Success – your plan should be divided into time domains which are termed macro-cycles, meso-cycles and micro-cycles. These cycles closely align to your goals providing the detailed framework of how and when you aim to deliver specific goals.

THE ROAD MAP

Having decided 'what' you are going to deliver based upon your determinants of success and your *wheel of success*, and having established your short-, medium- and long-term goals in the delivery of each determinant, you must now use your macro-cycle to map out 'when' you are going to deliver your outcome targets.

The macro-cycle is a timeline of the entire challenge from vision to delivery (and sometimes beyond if you have built in reflection and evaluation following the successful delivery of your challenge).

Imagine you are looking at a large-scale map of your plan. What you see is a long road with a series of towns indicating delivery dates for your short- and medium-term goals from the start to the delivery of the long-term goal of your challenge. The overall length of the road and therefore your macro-cycle will vary depending on the magnitude of your challenge, but it is generally measured in months to years. For Olympic athletes we often use a quadrennial (four-year) macro-cycle, while in business five- or ten-year macro-cycles are common. For personal challenges such as weight management I recommend using shorter macro-cycles of six to twelve months to ensure you allow enough time for meaningful change to occur while avoiding loss of motivation due to protracted timescales.

LOOK A LITTLE CLOSER

Having established your macro-cycle, imagine yourself using a smaller-scale map to take a closer look at it. Your macro-cycle is made up of a series of meso-cycles. Continuing our map analogy, the meso-cycle is a series of parallel lanes, each one dedicated to a specific determinant of success. A meso-cycle provides greater detail on 'what' you are going to deliver and 'when' you are going to deliver your outcome target, together with an overview of 'how' you intend to deliver each of your medium- and short-term goals.

In general, the length of meso-cycles tends to be measured in months. In business we tend to use three-month (quarterly) to six-month (half-yearly) meso-cycles, whereas in major sporting challenges we tend to use six- to twelve-week meso-cycles. Unlike the macro-cycle, the meso-cycle does not have to be a fixed period of time. For example, in elite Olympic sports we often use a longer base-conditioning meso-cycle (termed a 'winter' cycle for summer sports) of five months prior to a pre-season meso-cycle of three months and a competition meso-cycle of three months.

UNDER THE MICROSCOPE

Each meso-cycle is made up of a series of micro-cycles which provide details of 'how' you are going to deliver your short-term goals. This is the most detailed aspect of the planning process and makes up the task list for the prescription phase of our Profile-Prescribe-Monitor model. Because of the detail required at this stage of planning and the requirement to take into consideration your progress on an ongoing basis, the micro-cycle is prescribed on a short timescale, usually reflecting your monitoring programme for each determinant of success.

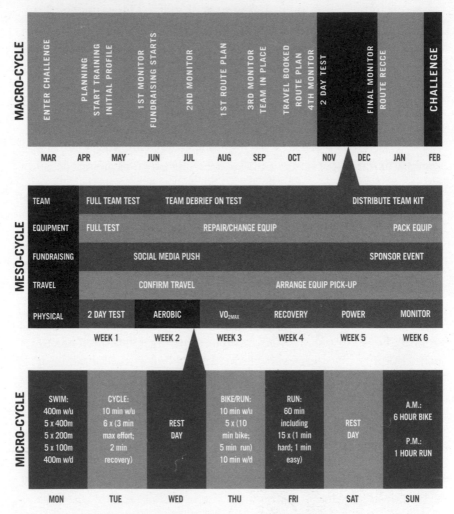

An example of a macro-, meso- and micro-cycle from a major bike challenge.

In general, I usually prescribe micro-cycles on a six-week cycle. This timescale allows enough time for adaptation to take place and ensure progress is in the right direction. Shorter micro-cycles can be used for those short-term goals that can be delivered rapidly. For example, if your short-term goal is to join a health club and complete an induction as part of your healthier lifestyle challenge, this can be achieved in a relatively short period of time, such as a week. In contrast, if your short-term goal is to reduce body-fat percentage by 3% it may take a six-week micro-cycle to deliver success.

GEAR CHANGE

Imagine your meso-cycles are like gear changes in your car. Your micro-cycles should deliver the increase in speed (improvement in performance) in a given determinant to enable you to change up through the gears at the start of each meso-cycle. By adopting this progressive approach to performance your journey will be much smoother. In contrast, if you attempt to change up more than one gear at a time, progressing too rapidly, you are likely to stall. It is often your *brain of success* which is in greatest danger of stalling as you struggle to cope with the excessive demands placed upon it. Profiling will enable you to identify what gear you are in for each determinant of success

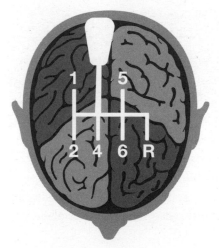

Gear change. Design macro-cycles to tackle each determinant of success one gear at a time to ensure you avoid stalling (or reversing).

111

(you will not always be in first gear) and prescribe the appropriate micro-cycles to deliver the right gear change at the end of your first meso-cycle. Trying to move up through the gears too quickly is not uncommon, particularly for those who have failed to design a detailed plan. Stalling slows your journey along the *road to success* and can sometimes lead to the selection of reverse gear, which can have a devastating impact on your *delivery of success*. Be realistic with your meso-cycle goals and ensure you change up one gear at a time.

TARGETED PRESCRIPTION

To optimize your micro-cycle prescription you should identify specific interventions which target the component parts of each determinant of success. Knowing the interventions which bring about the greatest gain in each component will result in a more rapid delivery of results and help to conserve your time and effort. This outcome-driven approach with attention to detail is the mark of excellence in the planning process. The more time you spend on targeting your prescription the greater the reward should be.

OUTCOME DRIVEN

Every time you work on your challenge there should be a pre-determined target outcome against which you can measure the success of the session. Each individual aspect of the micro-cycle should be outcome driven. The targeted outcome will help structure your work and ensure you remain focused on delivering to plan. This approach also enables you to better distribute your time and effort. A common mistake in physical preparation is to make every session as hard as possible. The outcome of this approach is a reduction in the quality of sessions due to fatigue, ultimately leading to mediocrity.

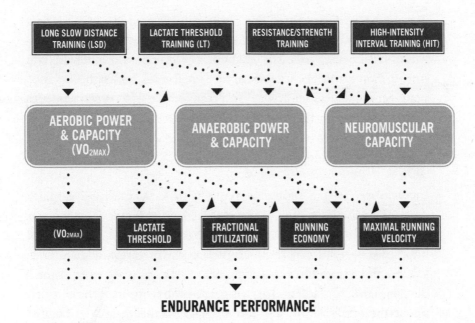

Targeted Prescription. Here is an example of the specific training interventions to enhance the component parts of the physical preparation determinant of success for an endurance running challenge. Different sessions target different components of performance.

Your micro-cycle planning is designed to deliver enhancements in specific elements of your determinants of success. Make sure you stick to plan to ensure you remain on the *road to success*.

IT'S ALL IN THE DETAIL

Make sure you pay attention to every aspect of performance during your planning phase, however small. A detailed analysis of all aspects of the challenge will enable you to predict and prevent any possible negative impact on performance. When looking to improve performance and deliver success, there are a number of mantras which have recently been popularized in elite sport. The concept of 'leaving no stone unturned' is an important approach which is often misunderstood. It does not mean only look under the big stones which have been previously linked to performance. Make sure you turn over *every* stone, including the small ones which others may not have looked under before. You must interrogate every aspect of performance, known or unknown, to ensure you avoid surprises.

▲▲ Challenge Highlight

In October 2010, I started working with Jon Smith on a major endurance challenge that would result in a historic ending. Jon was a fifty-six-year-old ex-professional footballer who had decided that he wanted to run a marathon – but he chose no ordinary marathon. Jon would attempt the North Pole Marathon, the coldest marathon on the planet. In addition to his age and having never attempted a marathon before, Jon was carrying significant injuries associated with his former career as a footballer.

Accordingly, the planning and preparation had to be meticulous. The physical preparation had to be targeted to ensure Jon was able to gain the greatest reward for his efforts while avoiding exacerbating his injuries. Taking an outcome-driven approach and managing Jon's physical limits to performance was critical in the management of his *brain of success*. Due to the changes in his injury status, as well as his work and family commitments, I was flexible in my approach to the micro-cycle prescription, constantly adjusting the programme to optimize outcome. Furthermore, we took a very detailed approach to equipment, ensuring that we minimized the impact and optimized performance.

In April 2011, Jon Smith became the oldest competitor to successfully complete the North Pole Marathon, and in doing so made history.

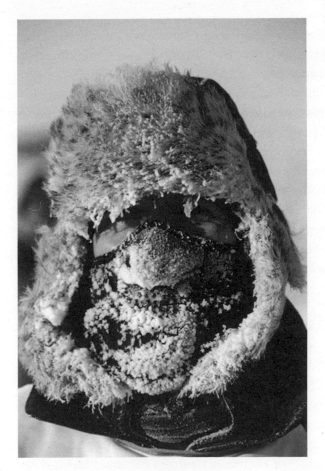

Jon Smith, 2011 North Pole Marathon finisher, the oldest in history.

TOUCH YOUR TOES

It is important to remember that your macro-, meso- and micro-cycles are not set in stone. Flexibility is the key to good planning, so be prepared to change your plans. Using the Profile-Prescribe-Monitor model (see Chapter 3 – The Wheel of Success) you will be able to mould your preparation in such a way that enables you to allocate your time, money and effort to the determinants which require greatest attention. Even the date of delivery of your long-term goal may need to be altered due to events beyond your control. This should not be viewed as failure. Remember, it is only a failure if you fail to learn from your experience.

My advice, however, is only to alter the delivery date of your long-term goal as a last resort. By adapting your meso- and micro-cycles you can often overcome setbacks and stick to your target time frame.

It is important to point out here that flexibility only works when it is used in response to monitoring results within a well-designed plan. You cannot make up for an underprepared, poorly executed plan by changing your meso- and micro-cycles on a continual basis. Poor planning is poor planning!

▲▲ *www.achievetheimpossible.co.uk*

TAKE CONTROL OF YOUR DESTINY

'Control the controllables' is another common mantra which is misinterpreted. There is no doubt that some factors of performance are uncontrollable; however, you should not ignore these factors and relinquish all control because there may be ways in which you can limit their impact. For example, if you are looking to improve your health you may not be able to control your genes but you can affect the way in which they work. We now understand that the way in which our genes work is, in part, associated with our behaviour. For example, your genetics may suggest that you have a propensity to be obese, but it is your behaviour patterns, your diet and level of physical activity which will determine whether or not your genes dictate your size or you take control and dictate your size. Making sure you have identified and planned for the uncontrollables will mean you are better prepared to deal with them and reduce the risk they may pose to the *delivery of success*.

PREPARATION

Having established your plan, it is now time to begin the preparation phase of your challenge. But be careful, it isn't simply a case of charging off in an uncoordinated fashion, working as hard as possible. Taking an intelligent approach to your preparation will lead to a smoother journey along your *road to success*.

INTELLIGENT WORKING

As discussed in Chapter 3 – The Wheel of Success, hard work creates the foundations upon which success is built. Without hard work those foundations are unlikely to support any of the structures you build on them, eventually leading, at best, to instability and, at worst, to the collapse of the entire challenge. There is no short-cut to hard work; nothing good comes easy. Accordingly, the first step in preparing for a challenge is to understand and accept that you and your team will need to commit to the work required to deliver success. However, it is important to remember that it is not just about working hard, it is also about working intelligently.

While it is undoubtedly true that the harder I work, the luckier I get, I also believe the more intelligently I work, the more successful I become. Working hard on areas that fail to bring about positive changes in your *wheel of success* is a waste of time, energy and money which only serves to increase your workload and reduce your motivation. Intelligent working is all about optimizing the resources you have at your disposal. We only have a finite amount of time, money and effort. Planning how you are going to partition these resources is crucial to optimizing performance. Attaching a value to each determinant of success before you start your preparation will provide you with a platform from which to work. For example, if you want to improve your health but only have a small amount of money with which to work, you should plan where best that money should be spent, in other words whether it is on gym membership or an improved diet.

PRINCIPLES OF PREPARATION

Once again, it's that place in the chapter where I add some science. This time it's coaching science, but bear with me because these concepts are pertinent to the preparation for all challenges, from lifestyle changes to business development. The following principles of preparation (in sport we call them the 'principles of training') provide the blueprint for optimizing your preparation.

- Specificity
- Progressive overload
- Reversibility
- Recovery

Specificity

The primary goal of training is to improve those determinants that impact on performance. Specificity refers to the targeting of preparation on specific determinants of success – in other words, those areas that impact on your *wheel of success*. In addition, your preparation must be individualized to your specific needs. A common mistake I see on a regular basis is the application of a generalized preparation phase which may result in enhanced performance but will always be sub-optimal. The reason people follow such programmes is usually because they have not truly identified their goal and so in many ways are hedging their bets. That's OK, but being OK at lots of tasks does not prepare you to be your best at one, especially as getting good in one area of performance often means that another area suffers. In other words, you can't be a sprinter and a marathon runner in the same week.

Progressive overload

In order to bring about change you must stress the system beyond what it is accustomed to. This 'overload' on the system must be progressively increased across time to ensure a continual adaptation. You can achieve a progressive overload by increasing the volume of work in three ways: intensity, frequency and duration. In other words, you can work harder, more often, or for longer. You can increase just one or all three factors to bring about progressive overload; however, the rate of change in progressive overload is important. If you progressively overload too slowly you may become disillusioned and lose motivation. On the other hand, if you overload too quickly you may burn out. Feedback from your monitoring will enable you to prescribe your optimal rate of overload.

Reversibility

Just as you adapt positively to a progressive overload, you will also regress if you reduce the volume of work. In sport we refer to reversibility as 'de-training', and in business it is often termed 'de-skilling'. Managing reversibility can create a number of issues in your preparation phase. For some, the fear of reversibility often leads people to work continuously without implementing recovery in the preparation phase. For others, the loss of performance following a period of reduced work leads to a loss of motivation and sometimes giving up on the challenge.

A classic example of this, again, is dieting for weight loss. While the dieter maintains calorie restriction and increased physical activity, they progressively lose weight, but as soon as they reduce their work rate by increasing calorie intake or reducing physical activity, reversibility kicks in and they will increase in weight. This is the commonest reason for de-motivation and failure.

Recovery

Recovery is fundamental to optimize positive change. By failing to recover, the quality of preparation falls, leading to a diminished progressive overload and poor-quality preparation. In some cases a lack of recovery leads to maladaptation resulting in a loss of performance. In sport I commonly see injury, illness and loss of performance associated with under-recovery. In fact there is a condition termed 'unexplained underperformance syndrome' (sometimes called 'overtraining syndrome'), which blights the lives of some elite athletes.

By planning your preparation phase using these principles of preparation you are more likely to deliver success. Of course, there are a number of other factors that will ensure your effort is rewarded with improved performance.

PERFECT PRACTICE MAKES PERFECT

'Practice, practice, practice' is a mantra you will often hear when looking to improve your performance. However, it is possible to work incredibly hard without gaining significant enhancements in performance if you are practising using a poor technique. In order to perfect your technique you must perform perfect technique in practice. This is true of any intervention, whether it's a golf swing, a lifestyle change or a new marketing campaign for business. A common mistake I often see is the rush to start working hard on a challenge without first identifying the best way to achieve success. Spending time early in a challenge designing, perfecting and executing a perfect intervention will optimize your chances of success, saving you time, effort and money. For example, with David Walliams's Channel swim, a great deal of attention was given to improving his swimming technique, particularly teaching him to breathe on both sides – a skill that is really important in open-water swimming. The consequence in the early stages was that his swimming was slower and he found trying to change his technique frustrating, but getting better at this skill was vital for the open-water training that came later.

DO THE THINGS YOU HATE WELL

As humans, our default programming leads us to take the path of least resistance – or in the preparation for a major challenge, the path of least work and greatest perceived enjoyment. This invariably means that we focus on the determinants of success we are good at and find the easiest, and therefore the ones we enjoy the most. One of the commonest mistakes I see is a focus of preparation on strengths often to the complete exclusion of weaknesses. The primary outcome of this approach is to enhance the strong determinants of success, resulting in little or no change to, and sometimes regression of, the weak determinants of success. Remember, success is optimized if you are able to move all determinants of success to the outer ring of excellence in your *wheel of success*.

MAINTAIN YOUR STRENGTHS AND OPTIMIZE YOUR WEAKNESSES

There is truth in the belief that you are only as strong as the weakest link, and having a major imbalance in your *wheel of success* will ultimately impact negatively on your performance. Following profiling, my approach is to focus on developing the weak determinants of success and maintaining strengths with the aim of achieving a greater balance of scores for all determinants of success. The timescale of delivering this balance rarely results in the simultaneous progression of all determinants of success. In other words, you cannot always change all determinants at the same time. During the preparation phase it is likely that each determinant will move at a different pace. The rate of change in a given determinant is often independent of other determinants; however, there may be a combined effect which leads to simultaneous progression of two or more determinants.

COMBINATION THERAPY

Having established separate meso-cycles for each of the determinants of success, it is important to remember that during the preparation phase you will be developing a number of determinants simultaneously. For example, a question I am frequently asked is, 'When do you input the psychological preparation?' The answer to this is simple: 'On a continual basis.' As we discussed in Chapter 4 – The Brain of Success, successfully delivering your short- and medium-term goals not only improves the targeted determinant of success, it also enhances your *brain of success* by supporting your belief that you can achieve your vision.

In addition to combining psychological determinants there are often a number of ways in which several determinants are positively affected by a single intervention. For example, if you are looking to enhance your health, physical activity will not only improve your physical performance, it will also improve your blood lipids and cholesterol profile, blood-sugar control and weight management. Planning interventions that provide combination therapy are incredibly productive and highly motivating.

SIZE ISN'T EVERYTHING!

Success is not built solely on large gains in single determinants of success. The accumulation of small gains across all determinants of success can make a real difference. We have spoken about how our *wheel of success* is composed of a number of determinants of success and how each of those determinants is made up of component parts. Now imagine that we improve each of these elements by just 1%. The accumulation of all these small improvements will culminate in an improvement in each determinant and together lead to a significant enhancement in performance overall.

The concept of 'marginal gains' has been popularized in recent times by elite sport; however, the philosophy of accumulating tiny improvements to deliver success is something that has been employed in all facets of life since time began. Whether it's business, lifestyle, health or sport, progressively improving every aspect of performance, even by a tiny amount, will ultimately lead to success.

NEVER ASSUME

Confidence is an important part of successful performance. In contrast, arrogance, leading to a belief that a challenge is easy or that you deserve success, is rarely a positive trait. It is worth remembering that if it was easy, everyone would do it! While detailed planning and preparation will increase confidence in your ability to deliver success, you should avoid assuming it is guaranteed. There will be moments during a challenge when you feel it is easier than expected. These are wonderful moments that should be stored in your memory to remind you how good it can be when things are a lot harder than expected.

A CHANGE IS AS GOOD AS A REST

On the journey to a major challenge there will be times when you feel you can't go on because of physical or psychological fatigue.

Psychological fatigue is often associated with task fatigue – boredom associated with repetition of the same task. Rather than taking time off and losing valuable preparation time, simply change your programme to focus on a different determinant of success. This is easily done by adjusting your micro-cycle programme. A common mistake is to beat yourself up by continuing a task with excessive fatigue, the result of which is poor-quality work and negative emotions.

JUST BECAUSE IT'S EXPENSIVE DOESN'T MEAN IT'S GOOD!

Another of the common mistakes I see on a regular basis is the belief that spending more money will guarantee success and reduce, or even eliminate, the requirement for hard work. Money is not a short-cut to success. For example, having a gastric band fitted costs a great deal of money and will deliver early weight loss, but surgery is not the answer in and of itself; hard work and a change of lifestyle, including diet and physical activity, is fundamental to long-term success. Making sure you spend your money intelligently on the right equipment, services and people for you and your challenge is far more important than the price.

Challenge Highlight

In February 2014, I trained the TV presenter Davina McCall to complete her 503-mile ultra-endurance triathlon from Edinburgh to London for Sport Relief. In addition to cycling 460 miles, summiting Scafell Pike and completing a half marathon fell run and a full marathon, Davina had to swim across Lake Windermere. All of this occurred in February in some of the worst weather conditions I have ever experienced on a challenge.

It was the 2km swim across Lake Windermere that posed the

greatest challenge. In addition to the almost freezing temperature of 4°C, swimming was the part of the challenge Davina most feared. Not being a strong swimmer and holding a lifelong fear of open water meant that Davina hated the prospect of getting in the water. In order to overcome what was undoubtedly her weakness determinant of success on her *wheel of success*, I focused a great deal of attention on doing the thing she hated well – something that at times placed a strain on training. In addition to working on the physical performance components, I focused closely on developing the psychological components based around fear, anxiety and confidence. With attention to detail I progressively developed her physical and psychological components in the pool until she was confident enough to take on an open-water session.

The primary aim of the open-water training session, Davina's first ever, was to overcome the fear and manage the anxiety which would ultimately increase her confidence. The training session was an incredibly traumatic experience. Davina had expressed her anxiety about open-water swimming but it was not until arrival at the lake for the training session that the magnitude of this fear was fully exposed. Davina was immediately in tears, expressing her belief that she could not complete the training swim. I continued to work closely with her, running through the meticulous plan which had been devised for the swim. I also discussed the 'If–Then' plan, which was extensive, taking every eventuality into account. The primary stimuli for Davina's anxiety were associated with her safety and her physical ability. The purpose of running through the 'If–Then' plan was to help manage her anxiety related to her safety and to reaffirm that she was in no danger. In tackling her physical ability I focused on positive affirmation of the incredible progress she had made in the pool and her undoubted ability to complete the training swim. Following a prolonged period of discussion and mentoring, Davina and I slowly entered the cold water to complete the 800m swim (less than half the distance of the Windermere challenge ahead of her). It was a traumatic process, but Davina made fantastic progress during her first open-water swim and as a result her fear, while not eliminated, was controlled.

On day 3 of Davina's 'Beyond Breaking Point' challenge we arrived on the western shore of Lake Windermere at seven a.m. Unlike the previous two days, during which we had endured a constant bombardment of rain, hail, sleet and snow, we stood under a cloudless blue sky in bright sunshine. The lake itself was still, not a ripple on its surface; it looked like glass. With the success of her training swim combined with ideal conditions it would have been easy for Davina, and the team, to assume success. However, Davina's lack of experience and the freezing temperature of the water meant that this section of the challenge remained her nemesis. As the start of the swim drew nearer, Davina's fear began to rise. In similar fashion to the training swim I worked closely with her to control her fear, drawing on her success in the training swim, her ability and her safety.

When the going gets tough . . . With meticulous planning and preparation, Davina McCall pushed herself beyond breaking point to raise £2.6 million and become a Comic Relief legend.

At 8.45 a.m., with much trepidation, we entered the water for what would become an iconic swim. Immediately the cold, combined with the anxiety and fatigue from the previous two days' efforts, led to Davina struggling to breathe. Swimming alongside her, I worked hard to maintain her focus on her belief that she could complete the swim. I set short-term goals which included completing a small number of strokes supported by positive affirmation that she was getting closer to her long-term goal of reaching the eastern shore of Windermere. After ninety minutes of incredible bravery, Davina was carried from the water, utterly fatigued, having successfully made the 2km crossing. She'd pushed herself to the limits of her capabilities and demonstrated the critical role that planning and preparation play in success.

www.achievetheimpossible.co.uk

TASK

At this point you have identified your vision (your challenge) and established your short-, medium- and long-term goals. Having established these key signposts you have identified the determinants of success and constructed your *wheel of success*. Your next tasks are as follows:

- Build your macro-cycle using your medium-term goals as signposts.
- Build your meso-cycles for each determinant of success for the first three months of your preparation.
- Build your micro-cycles for the first six weeks of your preparation for each determinant of success, including the target outcome for each episode of work.

CHAPTER SIX

THE TEAM OF SUCCESS

There's no 'I' in team but there is a 'ME'!

No matter what type of challenge you have set yourself, you will require a team around you to deliver success. For some of the large, complex challenges I have led, including those for Sport Relief and Comic Relief, it is obvious that a team is required to deliver success across all the determinants of success, including logistics, fundraising, media, etc. In fact some of these challenges required teams of over a hundred members; the Comic Relief 'Red Nose Climb' in 2009 had over 140! In contrast, you may think that losing weight or improving your health does not require a team. However, the importance of support in the planning, preparation and delivery of a challenge can be the difference between success and failure.

Selecting the best team should be directly linked to your *wheel of success* covering every determinant of success. Performance of the team is not solely associated with the knowledge or technical skills of individual team members. In fact, in my experience some of the best team members I have worked with have not been the most qualified. The ability to work as part of a team requires a range of skills which are not always taught but developed through experience. Of these skills, communication is of fundamental importance to performance. Communication is not only verbal (i.e. what we say and how we say it), it is also non-verbal (i.e. how we act). Both are powerful tools which if used effectively by all members of the team will ultimately dictate success. In addition to these attributes, every member of your team should have a *brain of success* to deliver your vision.

Having selected your team, you need to work hard to ensure

that each team member is fully integrated into the team. The early phase of integration is often a bumpy road with conflict around every corner. Making sure you identify potential problems early and take rapid and decisive action will ensure you create an environment in which every team member can deliver their best. Once fully integrated, you should develop an inter-disciplinary approach which, combined with the creation of team and personal leaders, will optimize the performance of your team, leading to the successful and enjoyable delivery of your vision.

Irrespective of the size of the team, the key to success is ensuring you select the best team, then create an environment that allows that team to integrate and perform to the best of its ability. There are a plethora of theories on optimizing team performance, but I find that my simple model of Selecting, Integrating and Performing is an effective way of delivering a *team of success*.

The *team of success*. Selecting the best team for your challenge, integrating individuals to operate as an effective team and creating an environment to optimize performance is the key to success.

By the end of this chapter you will have gained an understanding of:
- How to select the best team
  - The Team Tyre
  - The Team Filter
- The roles and responsibilities of team members
- Team selection in action
- The Race Across America (challenge highlight)

- How to integrate your team
- Working as a team
  - Multi-disciplinary to inter-disciplinary
- The importance of communication
- The development of personal leaders
- The importance of identifying problems early and creating solutions
- The importance of enjoyment in the *delivery of success*
- The Comic Relief Desert Trek (challenge highlight)

SELECTING: THE A-TEAM

Every challenge requires a team to optimize the *delivery of success*. While it is easy to see why some major challenges require a large team of support staff, a common mistake is to think that smaller, personal challenges do not require a team effort. Whatever your challenge you should look to appoint a team of specialists to support each of the determinants of success. Some challenges have fewer determinants of success and therefore require a smaller team, but none the less they do require a team.

For example, if you are looking to lose weight and you have identified physical activity and diet as your key determinants of success, you will need to identify a team to support you in delivering success in each of these areas. For physical activity you may appoint an exercise buddy and/or a personal trainer, and to look after your diet you may appoint a nutritionist or a weight-loss leader at a local Weight Watchers club. This may only constitute a team of three or four (including you, don't forget: even as leader you are a team member), but appointing the best team has been one of the critical elements in all the challenges I've worked on.

THE TEAM TYRE

Using your *wheel of success*, identify the key roles to which you will appoint a member of your team. The team creates a tyre of expertise around your *wheel of success* to ensure the smoothest and fastest journey on your *road to success*. At this point you should closely analyse exactly where you need support and establish how many team members you require to deliver success. It does not follow that the bigger the team, the greater the likelihood of success. A common mistake is to create a large team with poorly defined roles and not enough responsibility to maintain their *brain of success*.

Each member of the team should be appointed to a specific

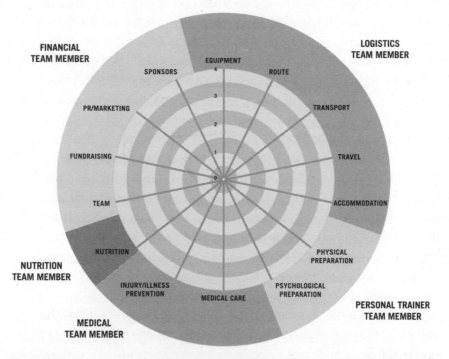

The Team Tyre. This example demonstrates the identification of five team members required to deliver success based upon the *wheel of success*.

role with clearly defined goals. Establishing discrete task responsibilities empowers team members, making them accountable for their contribution to the overall performance of the team. Rather than simply appointing a team member to every determinant of success, establish whether you could allocate more than one determinant. This will be based upon the attributes required for each role and successfully passing through the Team Filter (see below). Taking a streamlined, minimalist approach and only appointing team members that are absolutely required will make your task as leader much simpler and more productive.

THE TEAM FILTER

Selecting your team should be solely focused on delivering success. There is no place for sentiment in your criteria for team selection. You should not appoint team members just because you like them or because they have been recommended by a friend. You must seek those individuals who have the knowledge, technical skills and experience to deliver what is required for you to achieve your vision.

Aligning your team selection with your determinants of success will ensure that you optimize the delivery of excellence in each determinant on your *wheel of success*. Each member of your team should also have a *brain of success* that is focused on delivering your goals. You should choose candidates who love the challenge more than the kudos associated with being part of the project. Having team members who are happy to tell everyone that they are working with you to achieve your goals but in reality do very little to support you are of limited value.

Having established that your potential team member has the core skills of knowledge, technical skills, experience and a *brain of success*, the final, and most important, ingredient is communication. Team members need the communication skills to work as part of a

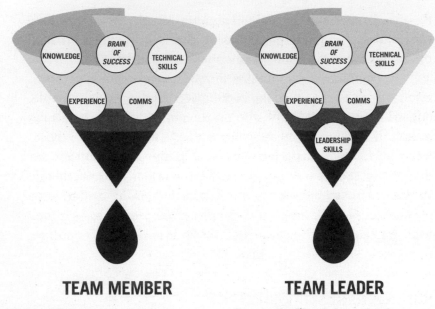

TEAM MEMBER

The Team Filter. Ensuring each team member has the knowledge, technical skills, experience, communication skills and a *brain of success* to deliver your vision is the first step in establishing your *team of success*.

TEAM LEADER

Team Leader Filter. In large, complex challenges you may need to appoint a team leader responsible for discrete areas of your *wheel of success*.

team and should be committed to working hard to deliver success not only in their specialist area but also for the team as a whole. Putting your potential team member through the Team Filter will enable you to identify the best team.

COMPLEX CHALLENGES

Larger, more complex challenges may require more than one team member working in a given area. For these challenges you may have to appoint a team leader responsible for coordinating the work of a specialist team focused on delivering specific areas of your determinants of success. When appointing a team leader you will need to add an additional screen to your Team Filter which assesses their leadership skills. By appointing a team leader you can reduce your workload, as the responsibility for overseeing the performance of your team across that area lies with that team leader.

Furthermore, appointing a number of team members in a given area should improve the breadth and depth of skills available, enhancing your *delivery of success*. Remember, big is not always beautiful, so do not increase your team size beyond what is absolutely necessary. Remain focused on establishing the best team for the job, not the biggest. In addition, as the leader of the challenge you must remember that you are responsible for the performance of your team leaders and as a consequence the team members they lead. Appointing a team leader is not an excuse for relinquishing responsibility; it is *your* challenge.

ROLES AND RESPONSIBILITIES

Selecting and creating a productive team requires the appointment of each team member to a clearly defined role. Having established a role covering each determinant of success for every member of your team, you should clearly define their responsibilities. Ensuring that each team member fully understands what they are accountable for, and giving them the autonomy to deliver, will increase their motivation and commitment to the challenge.

It is important to ensure that every team member understands the roles and responsibilities of other team members. In my experience, conflict between team members often arises when there is lack of role clarity. Make sure everyone knows what they should be doing and what everyone else should be doing. It is good to encourage cross-fertilization of ideas across the group, but you should be very careful to ensure that there are no crossovers in responsibilities. Ensuring that each team member has a discrete role is important in maintaining their *brain of success* and avoiding conflict.

TAKE AIM

With roles and responsibilities in place, you should set short-, medium- and long-term goals for each team member. Goals should not be created independent of the team member; they should be discussed and agreed to optimize commitment, belief and motivation. In large, complex challenges, goals are often task-specific and constitute only a part of your overarching goals. For example, imagine that a medium-term goal on your *road to success* is to raise £10,000 and, as part of that, a goal of one of your 'Financial Team' is to design a challenge website which attracts a thousand hits per day. These may look like unrelated goals but they are part of the same journey along your *road to success*.

In contrast, in personal challenges, your team's goals may align directly with your own goals. For example, if your vision is weight loss and your first short-term goal is to walk ten thousand steps per day, this will be the same goal as you would set your exercise buddy. Ensuring goal clarity for every team member is important in maintaining their *brain of success*.

Challenge Highlight

In June 2008, together with Richard Ball, Clive Middleton and Mathew Wilson, I was part of a team of four cyclists to enter the Race Across America (RAAM), a 3,000-mile non-stop cycling race from Oceanside, California to Annapolis, Maryland. The course travelled across the Rockies and the Appalachians with a cumulative climb from the Earth's surface to the stratosphere! Temperatures ranged from 40°C in the Mojave Desert to well below freezing on the 3,500m-plus summits of the Rockies.

Due to the large and complex nature of the challenge, and based upon the *wheel of success*, I established the need for a team of fifteen support staff including five team leaders: Logistics (Ady Green); Sport Science (Dr Richard Godfrey); Mechanical (Jam

Price); Medical (Peter Stratton); and Cycling Performance (me). Following the Team Filter and the Team Leader Filter, the fifteen exceptional individuals were appointed to the team, each with clearly identified roles and responsibilities. With the aim of a podium finish, the team reached Annapolis six days, ten hours and fifty-one minutes after leaving the Californian shores to finish in third position – an outstanding example of teamwork.

▲ *www.achievetheimpossible.co.uk*

The 2010 Race Across America (RAAM) team.

INTEGRATING: THE BUMPY ROAD

Now that you have established your team and assigned roles, responsibilities and goals, you must now develop an environment in which they can work together. Team integration can sometimes create the greatest amount of conflict within your team. You must be comfortable with disagreement and understand that it is part of the natural evolution of your team. That said, it is important that you identify the source of the conflict and deal with it rapidly and decisively to avoid slowing your journey. Sources of conflict are often associated with unclear roles and responsibilities which present themselves in three ways:

1. You have failed to clearly define the roles and responsibilities to either the team member or the rest of the team, which leads to confusion. You should identify the source of confusion and communicate with the team member and the entire team to ensure there is clarity on roles and responsibilities.

2. You have allocated the same responsibilities to more than one member of your team which leads to a loss of autonomy and a negative impact on their *brain of success*. You should identify where the crossover exists, alter the responsibilities and communicate the changes to the team members in conflict and the rest of the team.

3. One of your team members is not delivering to their goals due to low commitment and/or motivation which leads to frustration and conflict. There are a number of reasons why this may happen, including that the goal is too easy, too difficult, or it's perceived as of limited benefit to the challenge. You should establish the reason for the altered *brain of success*, identify a solution and communicate with the team member and the rest of the team.

While roles and responsibilities are a common cause of conflict in the integration of the team, you should not discount the fact that you may have been wrong in your team selection. This is not a failure in the formation of your *team of success* as long as you take responsibility and act rapidly and decisively to correct the matter. Invariably these issues are linked to innate factors that you cannot change. For example, the personality of your chosen team member does not allow them to work effectively with the rest of the team, or their circumstances have changed which does not allow them the level of commitment required to deliver success. Your Team Filter should identify many of these issues before you integrate the team; however, it may not be possible to predict some of these factors and you should be prepared to make changes to ensure the best *team of success*.

THE WHOLE IS ONLY AS GOOD AS THE SUM OF ITS PARTS

The performance of the team is based on each member of the team doing their best on a continual basis. It is therefore critical to optimize the performance of each member of the team irrespective of how small their role is. Making sure that each member of the team understands the importance of their role in delivering success is crucial in maintaining their *brain of success*. Every member of the team should understand and respect the contribution of other team members. Making sure that all team members feel valued will create a supportive environment in which success can thrive.

Cogs of Success. Ensuring that each team member is operating to the best of their abilities and maintaining support for their *brain of success* will lead to a successful team.

Monitoring progress and rewarding success on a regular basis help to reinforce the importance of each team member on an individual and team basis.

I like to think of the team as cogs in a machine. Some cogs may be larger than others, but the smooth running of the machine requires all cogs, big and small, to work in unison. The failure of one cog will ultimately lead to the failure of the entire system. Likewise, the failure of one team member, however small their task, has the potential to result in the failure to deliver a goal. Making sure that all team members are achieving the best that they can and ensuring you continually support them to maintain their *brain of success* will lead to the success of the team as a whole.

PERFORMING: WORKING TOGETHER

Having selected and integrated your *team of success*, you must now focus on the performance of the team. Appointing your team of specialists for each determinant of success is not in itself enough to ensure optimal performance. Your multi-disciplinary team must work together in an inter-disciplinary fashion in order to achieve success. One of the common reasons for team failure that I see on a regular basis is the appointment of experts who remain isolated, working independently of others. Creating these 'silos' of activity means there is very little cross-fertilization of ideas, leading to the poorly coordinated planning, preparation and delivery of a challenge. This lack of collaboration between team members results in slow progress along your *road to success*. Barriers and potholes are rarely predicted before they occur and solutions are hindered by a lack of communication.

Creating an inter-disciplinary team is sometimes more difficult than establishing your team in the first place. Bringing together individuals from different disciplines with varying degrees of expertise and experience takes a great deal of work to ensure optimal performance. The process of creating an inter-disciplinary team is often the most volatile period of team building and can lead to conflict, which will require your leadership. You should work hard to create a collaborative environment that engenders mutual respect across the team. Despite being diligent in your selection, you may need to change team members who have been unable to integrate fully into the team. Creating your inter-disciplinary *team of success* should be achieved as rapidly as possible to avoid major delays along your *road to success*. Act early and decisively to address any issues before they impact significantly on the *delivery of success*.

IT'S GOOD TO TALK

The ability to communicate is one of the most important skills of an effective team member. Communication is not solely about the ability to talk – there's nothing worse than a team member who talks non-stop, never listening to the input of others. Good communicators are able to get their point across in a way that everyone understands. The translation of technical knowledge and expertise into a language that is understandable by all is a real skill. Team members who insist on showing off their expertise by using complex language are of little use to a team.

In addition to talking, effective team members are able to listen and contribute constructively to discussions led by others. By creating mutual respect in this way you will improve the performance of your team. The use of multi-disciplinary team meetings to bring together your team members and provide them with an opportunity to share information is an important way to develop a productive inter-disciplinary team. These meetings should not be solely about information sharing. They should provide a forum for conversation and interaction between team members, which provides an opportunity to both support and criticize performance. Be careful not to allow only positive feedback. Criticism can be a valuable tool in enhancing performance if it is done in a constructive manner. Using your team to create solutions leads to a more rapid journey along your *road to success* compared to working in isolation.

PERSONAL LEADERS

Good leadership is crucial in optimizing the success of the team. In the next chapter – The Leadership of Success – I will examine your role as leader of your challenge in more detail. However, there are other aspects of leadership that operate within your *team of success*. In addition to the team leaders you may have appointed for a large, complex challenge, you should enable every member of your team to act as a leader to themselves: personal leaders.

Creating personal leaders is part of the process of developing intrinsic motivation. Creating autonomy and allowing each team member to be the leader of their own destiny is a potent stimulus in the development of their *brain of success*. In order to construct a team of personal leaders you need to create a supportive environment which provides each team member with the tools to optimize their development. In my experience, providing mentors who have established skills and experience in self-leadership is the most effective way of developing a team of personal leaders.

The level of support required will differ between team members. Some members of your team will rapidly become personal leaders while others will require significantly more support. The speed of progress to personal leadership is not necessarily an indication of quality but merely an expression of individual differences. To optimize the success of the team as a whole you must create an environment that allows every member of your team to be a successful personal leader and to perform to the best of their ability.

PREVENTION IS BETTER THAN CURE

Outstanding team members are not only able to solve problems, they should also prevent them from happening in the first place. Creating personal leaders allows team members to take a more proactive approach to deliver their goals. A proactive approach allows team members to see potholes in your *road to success* before you hit them and to create solutions to avoid them. This approach limits the impact of problems and maintains the speed of your journey. Working as a team creates better vision to see the potholes in advance and helps develop rapid solutions.

Your role as leader is instrumental in creating a proactive environment. If you are a micro-manager who takes control of every task, your team will be reluctant to take a proactive approach. Equally, if you are too laissez-faire, your team may not have an environment that enables them to see into the future. As leader you must create an environment where personal leaders are able to work in an inter-disciplinary way to prevent problems before they occur.

DON'T FORGET TO SMILE

Being part of a successful team should be an enjoyable experience. As we have already discussed, there will be hurdles, potholes and occasional 'dark times' along the *road to success*, but these should be outweighed by the fun times along the way. Some of the enjoyable moments occur spontaneously; however, it is always important to build in fun times along your *road to success* to ensure that every member of your team and your team as a whole experiences the lighter side of the challenge.

Rewarding the success of achieving goals is only part of your enjoyment plan, as rewards often focus on individuals. You should plan team events to share enjoyable experiences and provide an environment where the team can get to know each other and better understand the roles and responsibilities of every member of the team. These events will create positive reinforcement of your shared vision, support the maintenance of their *brain of success*, and improve the performance of your team. Remember, memories of misery are short-lived, but the memories of good times last for ever.

Challenge Highlight

In March 2010, I led a group of nine celebrities on the Comic Relief Desert Trek, a five-day 100km walk across the Kaisut Desert in eastern Kenya: radio and TV presenter Dermot O'Leary; musicians Olly Murs and Craig David; TV presenter Lorraine Kelly; radio presenters Scott Mills and Peter White; comic actress Ronni Ancona; actress and TV presenter Nadia Sawalha; and actress Kara Tointon. The group ranged in age from early twenties (Olly Murs) to mid-sixties (Peter White), with a broad spread of physical abilities, highlighted by Peter White, who is blind.

This eclectic mix of individuals, all devoid of any ultra-endurance walking experience, required a very carefully selected team of specialists to deliver success. Having established the determinants of success for this unique challenge and working closely with Comic Relief, the BBC and the ExMed trekking team in Kenya, we used the Team Tyre and *wheel of success* to ensure that a team was appointed to cover every determinant of success.

Each potential team member was subject to the Team Filter and successful candidates were appointed to the team. It is not uncommon at this stage to eliminate candidates; however, careful selection of potential team members prior to passing them through the Team Filter reduces the rejection rate, which improves the speed of selection and limits the damage related to being unsuccessful. On this occasion we sadly had to lose a highly skilled, experienced member of the communications team due to their insulin-dependent diabetes, which could not be successfully supported in such a remote location. Establishing this limitation early in the process was important in limiting the damage to the team and the individual, and it also allowed sufficient time to appoint a high-quality replacement.

For such a large and complex challenge delivered by multi-agencies it was clear that team leaders would be required to cover specific areas of the challenge. Following evaluation through the Team Leader Filter, leaders were appointed to the trekking team; the Comic Relief social-media, fundraising and artist-liaison teams; the BBC documentary team; and the BBC radio team. As a result, in addition to the nine celebrities, thirty specialists were appointed to the team, coordinated by six team leaders.

Optimizing the performance of such a disparate group of high-quality individuals, each with their own goals, is an incredibly complex task that always results in a bumpy *road to success*. This is despite the development of detailed roles and responsibilities which are communicated to the team on a continual basis, starting during the planning phase and continuing through to the completion of the challenge. The extremely high-pressure environment – failure is simply not an option in these high-profile challenges – combined with exhaustingly long days in an extreme environment (remember, the entire team had to complete the 100km alongside the celebrities while carrying out their specialist role) often led to conflict between team members. Strong team leadership and overall leadership were required to ensure these bumps in the *road to success* did not evolve into potholes or even 'dark times'. The majority of these conflicts were resolved in the daily multi-disciplinary team meetings, with the remaining conflicts taken up on a more personal one-to-one basis.

In addition, extreme conditions can, on occasions, lead to team members being unable to complete their roles. This was true of this challenge where, on a number of occasions, the 40°C-plus temperatures led to members of the media teams, who were carrying and operating heavy equipment, collapsing with heat exhaustion and becoming unable to carry out their specialist roles. In these situations team leaders needed to act rapidly and decisively to appoint responsibilities to other team members and ensure that crucial media tasks were completed as planned.

Every member of the team must be working at their very best to ensure the overall success of the team, irrespective of their or others' perception of how important the role is. This was best demonstrated to me by our stills cameraman, Tim Allen, who was an absolute genius with a camera. While there may be a perception that stills photography is less important than other areas of performance, the truth is it plays a crucial inter-disciplinary role in these challenges. The pictorial diarizing of the challenge is not only important following the completion of the challenge; it now plays an instrumental role in real-time reporting of the challenge.

This real-time ability supported the crucial work of social-

The 2010 Comic Relief Desert Trek team.

media specialist Mark Woods, not only in communicating the story but also in providing a platform to raise money – definitely the most important part of a Comic Relief challenge. Ensuring Tim was able to operate at his best at all times and to respond to rapidly changing events was instrumental to the overall success of the challenge. This was particularly true when Peter White, the sixty-three-year-old blind radio presenter, collapsed with heat exhaustion and severely damaged feet on day 3. As with all of these challenges, the sight of a celebrity in misery reported instantly across social media with graphic images results in a huge swell of public support, leading to a massive spike in donations. Making sure every cog in your machine is working to the best of their abilities is the key to the *team of success*.

▲ *www.achievetheimpossible.co.uk*

TASK
- Using your *wheel of success*, write down how many team members you require.
- Write down a detailed list of responsibilities for each member of your team.
- Using your Team Filter, identify your team members.
  - If your challenge is large and complex use the Team Leader Filter to identify team leaders and write down a detailed list of responsibilities for each leader.
- Identify key times to bring your team together for multi-disciplinary team meetings and write them down on your *road to success*.
- Along your *road to success*, write down the plan of enjoyable team events.

CHAPTER SEVEN

THE LEADERSHIP OF SUCCESS

Control your own destiny

The subject of successful leadership has been analysed, discussed and written about for millennia. A plethora of books dedicated to leadership are available on the shelves; management courses across all disciplines from sport to banking feature at least a component on leadership. To that end, I do not intend to cover the ocean of information currently out there, only to give my personal experience of leadership which may in part cross over with existing thinking but will hopefully provide some new ideas for anyone taking on a major challenge.

In life we are led to believe that only a small number of leaders exist, with the rest simply following. This is particularly true in sport where there is a common perception that there are only a few leaders within a team – the captain and the manager or performance director, for instance. In reality, every member of a team is a leader whose responsibility it is to deliver their optimal performance to ensure the overall success of the team, however small their task.

Coordinating these individual parts and optimizing the performance of a team is far from easy and requires good leadership. There are a variety of leadership styles, but the primary role of the leader is to create an environment where every team member can reach their full potential. In order to do this a good leader is able to develop the *brain of success* of each team member. To achieve this there are a number of facets to leadership that a good leader must optimize to deliver success.

By the end of this chapter you will have gained an understanding of:
- The elevator pitch of your vision statement
- Leading from the front while being behind the scenes
- The delegation of tasks while remaining responsible and accountable
- The role of multi-disciplinary team meetings
- The language of leadership
- Variable leadership approach
- Rewarding success
- Emotional leadership
- Helen Skelton's South Pole trek (challenge highlight)
- Reflective practice
- The Million Pound Cycle (challenge highlight)

WHY USE A HUNDRED WORDS WHEN ONE WILL DO?

Your first task as a leader is to assemble the best team possible. In order to do this you must be a good salesperson, able to sell your vision in such a way that it attracts the right people to deliver success. In order to inspire potential team members you must create a pitch that brings people with you. As a leader you must have a clearly stated long-term goal. This is the bait that will attract the team and as such it should be immediately obvious when you begin your recruitment process.

Having established the interest of potential team members, you must create a vision statement outlining the how, when and why of your vision. Your vision statement should be clear, concise and inspiring. Long, drawn-out statements which are ill-conceived and poorly structured will immediately lose the interest of your potential team member, and once lost it may prove difficult to re-engage with your first-choice team member, which may mean having to settle for second best – not a great start to delivering success! The vision statement should not only be an inspirational goal for you as leader, it should also inspire the team by providing individually challenging goals leading to personal experience, development and achievement.

GOING UP

The commonly used 'elevator pitch' is a great way of constructing your vision pitch. Imagine you are in an elevator with a potential team member who is critical to the *delivery of success*. You have thirty seconds to sell your vision to them and bring them on board as a team member.

Here's an example of a pitch you might use if you are looking to lose weight and need to recruit an exercise buddy:

'My long-term goal is to lose 42lb (20kg) and fit into the size 12 dress I wore on my honeymoon. Over the past three years I have progressively increased my weight through a combination of poor eating habits and lack of exercise. My increased weight has changed me as a person and I do not like what I have become. That is why I have set myself this goal which I intend to deliver in six months. I am highly motivated and fully committed to delivering the goal. I know that I cannot achieve this goal alone and that I need the best team around me to deliver success. That is why I would like you to be my exercise buddy because you are an incredible motivation to me. As my exercise buddy you will be one of the key drivers of success. Exercising together we can both improve our fitness, have fun and get me into my favourite size 12 dress for the first time in three years.'

Alternatively, here's an example of a pitch you might use if your aim is to complete a major physical challenge and you need a mentor:

'I have always loved running and have held a lifelong dream of running a marathon. Since starting work and having a family I have given up running, and exercise in general, and become very unfit. As a result mine and my family's quality of life has diminished because I have lost my motivation for activity. Even playing with my children has become a chore! That is why I have set myself the goal of running the London Marathon in nine months' time. I believe I can achieve my goal and am highly motivated and fully committed to crossing the finishing line. To make my dream come true I need the best team around me. As an experienced marathon runner and a real inspiration to me I would like you to be my mentor. Your knowledge, expertise and experience is crucial for me to be successful and I hope that together we can achieve my lifelong dream of running a marathon.'

YOU ARE WHAT YOU DO, NOT JUST WHAT YOU DID

We have all met the leader who takes every opportunity to tell us what they achieved in the past; how good they used to be! There is no doubt that what we did moulds us into what we currently are. However, it is erroneous to believe that what once made us successful will continue to deliver success. In my opinion, great leaders lead by example. The days of the socio-economic hierarchy of a century ago are long gone. As a contemporary leader you cannot expect to sit miles behind the lines while your team put their lives on the line to deliver your vision. You must be prepared to work at the coalface, to demonstrate your commitment to delivering success. You must lead from the front.

In order to do this you should work hard on gaining the trust of your team. You must have credibility, which is based not only on what you have done in the past but also your current abilities. Having established your credibility and gained the respect of your team you should be motivational and inspirational if you are to bring the team with you and optimize their performance along the *road to success*. Without this approach you will be unable to create a fully functioning, cohesive team able to consistently deliver success.

THERE'S NO POINT HAVING A DOG AND BARKING YOURSELF

A word of caution when it comes to leading from the front: you should be careful not to assume that you can do everything yourself. If it was that simple, you wouldn't need a team; and if this is the case it probably isn't a real challenge! We have already outlined the importance of the *team of success* but it is you as the leader who is responsible for optimizing the function of the team.

There are two scenarios of unsuccessful leadership that I commonly see. First is the 'one-man band'. These are the leaders who think they can do everything themselves. They tend to avoid appointing a team, assuming they have all the skills necessary to deliver success. Sadly, this is rarely, if ever, the case and invariably leads to failure. The second scenario is the 'control freak'. This is the leader who appoints a team of specialists but insists on taking over every task. This lack of delegation leads to a host of negative outcomes and, almost inevitably, failure. The success of the vision is built around the success of the team. Accordingly, having appointed the best team you should allow them to do what they do best (which is always better than you!).

DELEGATION, THAT'S WHAT YOU NEED

Your key role as leader is to delegate responsibility for the delivery of the various aspects of the challenge to each member of the team.

You should clearly articulate the job of each team member and ensure they understand what is expected of them. In addition, it is important that all team members understand what each other is responsible for. In delegating responsibility you are empowering each team member, allowing them to feel like they are playing an important part in delivering success. This empowerment of ownership develops their *brain of success* by creating an intrinsic motivation which will provide them with the belief that they can deliver success and drive them on to commit fully to the challenge.

In order to ensure that all team members work to the best of their ability, you should monitor performance on a regular basis and reward success. Rarely will the journey along your *road to success* be a smooth one. There will be occasions when the *brain of success* of some of your team is working sub-optimally. A partial loss of commitment, belief and/or motivation can lead to reduced performance. As a leader I do not believe that you should punish this behaviour; instead work hard to incentivize a change in behaviour. This is particularly true when your team is working for free!

STAY IN CONTACT

Delegation does not mean relinquishing your responsibilities as leader. It is your challenge and as such you remain fully accountable for every step along the journey. There is nothing to be gained from disowning any aspect of planning, preparation and delivery. A common mistake is to give a team member full responsibility of a determinant of success for which you are poorly motivated. Giving up responsibility does not lessen the determinant's importance. Equally, being able to blame someone else for failure will do little to deliver you success. The overall responsibility for delivering success remains with you and as such you must have a complete overview of all aspects of the challenge on a continual basis. You are responsible for the central coordination of the work; ensuring that all team members are fully informed of progress across all areas of the challenge; implementing the output of work produced by the team; and, ultimately, delivering the challenge. Accordingly, you should work harder than any single member of the team coordinating the challenge and ensuring the *delivery of success*.

Take as an example that your long-term goal is to improve your health and one of the determinants of success is creating a better work-life balance. You cannot simply appoint your PA to the team and delegate the coordination of your diary if you do not take responsibility for overseeing the work, checking your diary on a regular basis and adhering to the changes made.

THE LEADERSHIP ENGINE

Real gains can be made from strategically placed, well-planned meetings which have clear objectives and outcome goals. Multi-disciplinary team meetings can be an incredibly valuable tool in optimizing the function of your team when these principles are followed. Getting your team together regularly to share information, monitor progress and recognize achievements, identify issues early and create solutions, and establish the next phase of work is a very important way of maintaining the *brain of success* of each team member. Meetings with the entire team provide regular opportunities to reinforce your vision and belief in the team's ability, and enhance motivation, ensuring a continued commitment to the *delivery of success*. Leading multi-disciplinary team meetings to ensure they are rapidly executed, delivering maximum benefit, is an important skill for a good leader. The multi-disciplinary team meeting provides the catalyst for a truly inter-disciplinary team approach – the essence of a successful team.

Imagine the team is an engine and each team member is a

cog in the machine. The leader acts as the central cog which drives the engine. The leader has contact with all team members and in turn each team member understands and recognizes the work of the other members of the team. The central role of the leader is to maintain the perpetual motion of the team to ensure progress towards the success.

The Leadership Engine. A truly inter-disciplinary team approach has the leader central to all determinants of success and ensures that multi-disciplinary team meetings provide an environment for the team to work as a single engine driving the *delivery of success.*

THE CENTRAL GOVERNOR

In my opinion one of the toughest but most important jobs of a leader is to optimize the function of the *brain of success* in all team members. As with your own *brain of success*, the team's commitment, belief and motivation will vary throughout the challenge and it is therefore important that you monitor your team on a continual basis. You must be attentive to all team members to identify problems early and provide solutions rapidly if performance is not to be significantly affected. In my experience it is rarely technical skills or knowledge that limit performance, it is commitment, belief and motivation that demonstrate the greatest variability and require the greatest support.

In addition to supporting the *brain of success* for each of your team members there will be times during a challenge when your own *brain of success* will be put into question. It is of paramount importance that you only display this to those members of the team you have entrusted with the responsibility of supporting you in this area. You should avoid voicing your loss of commitment, belief and/or motivation to the entire team as this can create an increase in fear of failure across your team, which leads to a slowing of your journey along your *road to success*. Selecting which member of your team you use to support your *brain of success* is not a simple task. All members of your team have passed through the Team Filter and have demonstrated experience in their specialist area, but it is often those team members who have extensive experience of delivering success in major challenges and with whom you have a close relationship who are likely to be the best candidates for the role.

IT'S NOT WHAT YOU SAY, IT'S HOW YOU SAY IT

For me, one of the most important qualities of successful leadership is communication. The language you use to communicate your message is of paramount importance in motivating your team to continue working hard on delivering success. Being a good communicator is, in part, a skill you are born with; however, it is also a skill that can be developed. Understanding each team member and how best to communicate with them on an individual basis is a valuable skill. You should work hard at understanding the emotional needs of each team member and vary your approach accordingly.

It is amazing how much you can get out of someone if you can communicate effectively with them. Try to take a balanced approach to the importance of the challenge. You should avoid taking a serious approach on a continual basis. Having a sense of humour is important, but you should ensure you use it appropriately and at the right time to optimize its effect. At the end of a challenge you will remember only the fun times so it is important as a leader that you ensure the team are able to fully appreciate them as and when they happen.

FLEXIBILITY

Each team member will experience a different journey along your *road to success*. Differences ranging from the speed of travel to the number of times each member needs to pull over to refill their fuel tank of motivation mean that a good leader adopts a flexible path to the long-term goal. Being able to accommodate strengths and weaknesses is important if you are to get the best out of each member of your team. Accordingly, you should be able to vary your leadership approach depending on the situation and the individual. You should understand that your plan is not set in stone, and evaluate progress and adapt your plan as necessary. Furthermore, communication skills play an important role in optimizing the performance of each team member and you should adapt your approach to ensure you are engaging optimally with each team member. Your aim is to create an atmosphere of respect for individual differences and to ensure that all members of the team understand that everyone is doing their best to deliver success.

ACCELERATE, MAINTAIN, REWARD

As leader you should be monitoring each team member on a regular basis and comparing their progress against the performance goals you have established for them along the *road to success*. This is not a micro-management 'tick box' exercise, but you do need to say 'well done', and to do that you need to be able to recognize the effort put in, and you can only do that when you know how your team's performing. The objective of this monitoring process is threefold: to support and accelerate, to maintain, or to reward.

For team members who are struggling to deliver their goal, you should provide support to ensure they are able to achieve success in a timely fashion. For team members who are on course to deliver success, you should provide encouragement to maintain their *brain of success*. For team members who deliver their goal, you should celebrate their success and reward them publicly. The task of over-seeing the work of your team requires a continual effort, twenty-four hours a day, seven days per week. This may appear an onerous task, but it should not be carried out solely by the leader as it is likely to cause burnout; the leader needs systems in place to help her or him recognize achievements. Overseeing work in this way will help create an environment within which every team member works to achieve their best. This in turn ensures the smoothest and fastest journey along the *road to success*.

A FAMILY AFFAIR

I like to think of a team as being a family. As leader you are head of the household, which is not an easy task. In order to achieve the smooth running of the house you are not only responsible for the more mundane aspects of finance, nutrition, cleaning, repairs, etc. You are also responsible for emotional leadership – coordinating the family (team) and creating a sense of belonging (team membership). It is imperative that you create an environment of caring for each team member. A team is made up of individuals and as such you should take an individual approach to supporting each team member.

Obvious elements such as knowing each team member's name can make a real difference – not knowing their name can create major issues. Knowing nicknames can create a real sense of belonging. Understanding what motivates each team member and using specific references to them in conversation leads to a caring and supportive environment. You should recognize the limitations of each team member and help support them to achieve to the best of their ability. Reassuring team members that they are an important part of the team creates an environment to optimize performance.

◢◣ *Challenge Highlight*

In December 2011, TV presenter Helen Skelton reached the South Pole having walked, skied, kitesurfed and cycled across the Antarctic. This was an enormous project requiring a huge team including a large number of team leaders from a range of specialities in fields such as performance, TV, adventure, environment and fundraising. For such large teams to work optimally they often take on the feel of a family unit. Strong leadership combined with effective communication is crucial in optimizing the performance of the family unit and maintaining the *brain of success* of each member of the team. With each member of this team working at 100%, Helen was able to focus on her performance and deliver success in one of the toughest environments on the planet.

 www.achievetheimpossible.co.uk

On the bottom of the world! Helen Skelton is a true action woman. Having canoed the length of the Amazon in 2010, she walked, skied, kitesurfed and cycled to the South Pole in 2012.

YOU'RE NOT ALWAYS RIGHT

We have accepted that the *road to success* is not always smooth. In addition to the barriers, potholes and occasional 'dark times' there will be moments when you simply get it wrong. Accepting when you are wrong and admitting to it publicly is an important step in building trust with your team. A common mistake is for leaders to assume that admitting they are wrong will reflect badly on them and they will lose the support of their team. In reality, concealing the fact that you have made a mistake or, worse still, blaming others, can be more damaging than admitting getting it wrong.

The key to dealing with these problems is to take rapid and decisive action to ensure you limit the damage. By taking control of the situation you will increase the confidence of your team in your leadership. Of course, you cannot continually get things wrong if you want your team to follow you. Invariably, repeat offenders are those who have failed to plan or have not fully developed their *brain of success*. Rather than continue, you should revise your plan to smooth your *road to success* and revisit your *brain of success* to ensure you have optimized your commitment, belief and motivation.

BEHIND THE SCENES

When working on major challenges for television I spend much of my time behind the camera. As a leader you must be comfortable with this anonymity while allowing the credit to go to the performer(s). Even when it is your personal challenge, there will be times when you have to stand in the background as members of your team take the credit for delivering success. For example, if you are taking part in a charity cycle ride and one of your team has built an incredible website which will be instrumental in reaching your fundraising target, you should not only stand aside to allow them to take the credit for their work but, as leader, you should be championing their cause to ensure maximum public recognition.

In contrast, as leader you must take responsibility for problems and mistakes. A common mistake made by unsuccessful leaders is to take all the credit for successes and have sloping shoulders when it comes to failures, blaming others for their inadequacies. Great leaders are often invisible, only seen when they are defending their team when mistakes are made. Even when it is your personal challenge you must recognize your role in taking responsibility for your own destiny.

LOOKING BACK

Reflective practice provides a tool to mould and develop your knowledge and skills as a leader. Reflection on what you do allows you to better understand the reasons for success or failure of a particular intervention or relationship. In my opinion, excellence is achieved when you are able to critically analyse performance and make the necessary, and sometimes difficult, changes required to deliver success. Failure is most often seen in those who believe they are always right; an absence of introspection and self-evaluation is a flaw uncommon in the best leaders. That said, self-reflection is significantly strengthened through the support of your team.

Reflective practice should not only focus on success or failure but how you got there. Understanding which elements of

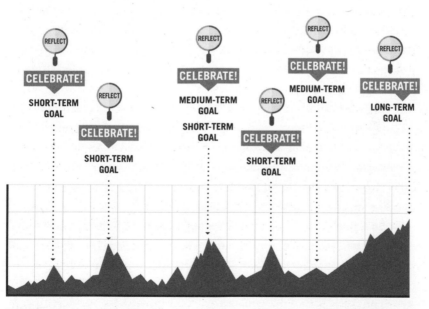

Reflective practice. Alongside your celebrations you should ensure you reflect on the positive and negative aspects of reaching your goals and use the outcome to inform your future journey along the *road to success*.

an intervention worked and which didn't will allow you to replicate success and reduce future problems. Just because you were successful in reaching a short-term goal does not mean you cannot improve. Equally, failing to reach a short-term goal does not put the entire challenge in jeopardy if you identify the problems and create solutions. Working with your team to evaluate your progress along your *road to success* is a task that takes time and effort but is well worth it in the long run.

THE REAR-VIEW MIRROR

Using your Mountain of Success you have already established your short-, medium- and long-term goals and appointed a celebration to the successful delivery of each goal. Having celebrated, you should now use your rear-view mirror to reflect on your achievement. Alternatively, you should complete the process of reflective practice at the point of failure in any goal. It is important to remember that reflecting on success and establishing why you were successful and what could have been improved is as important as reflecting on failure.

It is not uncommon to spend too much time dwelling on failure. While analysing the reasons for failure and establishing solutions to avoid future failure is a critical step in your journey along your *road to success*, you should avoid dwelling on the past. Once you have developed a new plan for delivering your goal you should park your failed vehicle and move on without delay. This rapid development of a new plan will allow your *brain of success* to focus on a positive goal rather than wallow in the quagmire of failure. In contrast, you should spend more time reflecting on success compared with failure, as reflecting on failures and developing solutions is usually more effective following success and can provide far greater support for your *brain of success*.

The process of reflection is feedback and feed-forward.

Feedback is derived from you and your team to identify what went well and what went wrong. You should then identify solutions to problems and strategies to maintain or enhance each successful aspect of delivery. You should then feed-forward the solutions into future actions to deliver future success. Below is an example of a reflective grid highlighting the use of the feedback and feed-forward processes.

Goal	Determinant of success	What went well	What went wrong	ACTION: What actions you are going to take to ensure future success
Short-term Goal 2: Successful loss of 14lb in 12 weeks	Alcohol consumption	Stuck to zero alcohol consumption during the week		1. Excellent work, maintain commitment during the week
			Consumed over 15 units on a regular basis at the weekend, usually associated with partner pushing the alcohol consumption	2. Make a personal contract to limit weekend consumption; ask partner to make their own personal contract to support you in delivering your goal
	Physical activity	Physical activity target for daily walking steps (15,000) reached		3. Set new goal of 20,000 steps per day by building an extra 30 minutes of walking in 3 × 10-minute bouts across the day
			Physical activity target for three gym sessions per week rarely achieved due to lack of motivation	4. Identify an exercise buddy who can commit to going to the gym with you three times a week; write a personal contract with your exercise buddy to ensure you meet this target

	Diet	Maintained an average of 1,500 calories per day	Large fluctuations in calorie consumption between days due to over-consumption associated with chocolate and alcohol consumption at the weekends	5. In addition to reducing weekend alcohol consumption set in Target 2, remove all chocolate from the house and do not buy any more
	Brain of success	Remained motivated and committed to delivering the target throughout – I continue to believe I can reach my long-term goal		6. Excellent *brain of success*. Keep up the good work and you will achieve your long-term goal!
			Lost focus on the weekends regarding alcohol and calorie consumption combined with low motivation for gym sessions	7. Focus on delivering Targets 2, 4 and 5. Ensure that you concentrate on your *brain of success* at the weekends. Write large public notices reminding you of your goals and place them strategically around the house (i.e. on the fridge, cupboards, wine rack, etc.)

The reflection grid. Using feedback to establish what went well and what went wrong in the delivery of a goal, followed by feed-forward to identify what actions should be taken to ensure future success.

THE WORLD IS FULL OF EXPERTS!

In my experience, whenever you take on a major challenge there is always a plethora of people who have done it before, or who know someone who has done it before, or who have read a book about it, or who know someone who can help, etc., etc. This pseudo-expert opinion comes from everyone you speak to about the challenge. In fact, opinions and advice can be forthcoming without even mentioning the challenge!

This almost constant bombardment of information can be confusing and often leads to deviations from your planned *road to success*. While it is tempting either to take on board all the advice or ignore it completely, the real skill of a good leader is to filter out the noise and identify quality. As leader you must be confident in your decisions and project that confidence to your team. In order to optimize your speed of travel along your *road to success* you should avoid making changes midway to delivering your short-term goals. Holding firm on your Profile-Prescribe-Monitor model will enable you to identify mistakes much easier than making constant changes to your preparation. Making measured changes to your plan based on the best information possible is the mark of a good leader.

 ## Challenge Highlight

In March 2010, I led a team of seven celebrities taking on a 1,000-mile cycle ride from John O'Groats (the most northerly mainland tip of Scotland) to Land's End (the most southerly tip of England) in aid of Sport Relief. The challenge was titled 'The Million Pound Cycle' in honour of the sum the challenge aimed to raise. The team included actor, comedian and writer David Walliams; actor and comedian Miranda Hart; TV presenter Davina McCall; comedian and radio presenter Patrick Kielty; radio and TV presenter Fearne Cotton; and comedians Russell Howard and Jimmy Carr.

This was a non-stop challenge for which I had set the goal of completing the 1,000 miles at 77 hours (a formidable 13mph average across the toughest terrain in the UK during winter). In addition to the extensive determinants of success for such a complex challenge, the non-stop nature of the event meant there was a greater chance of potholes and 'dark times' along the *road to success*. Furthermore, the very different skill levels, physical conditioning and personalities of the celebrities would mean a significant challenge for me in optimizing their *brain of success* and creating an environment conducive to success. The skill levels of the celebrities ranged from highly experienced on a bike (Davina, Russell and Patrick) to having never ridden a road bike before (Miranda). In line with their bike-handling skills, their physical capacities were also vastly different. The one aspect of the challenge where they did have an allegiance was their experience of multi-day ultra-endurance events, which was none!

Despite the significant differences in cycling performance it was critical for me to develop an environment of trust where each team member recognized that everyone was working to the best of their ability for the team. Because of the weather, the terrain and the time of day (cycling in the dark is very different from cycling in daylight), combined with the variance in ability, some team members had to travel significantly faster than the 13mph average required to deliver success. This meant the onus of responsibility to work incredibly hard to make up time during the most difficult periods of the journey (at night, in the snow, over mountainous terrain) was placed on certain team members (i.e. Davina, Patrick and Russell).

Ensuring that their commitment was rewarded publicly by announcing their average split times to the entire team, on social media and radio, was important in maintaining their *brain of success*. It was also important to recognize the success of all team members, and by setting target speed and distance goals for each episode of cycling we were able to recognize and reward success across the team.

Being able to take a different approach to leadership was of paramount importance during this challenge. Not only did the individual members of the team have different personalities and respond differently to leadership, they also responded very differently to the environments they faced throughout the challenge. The non-stop nature of the challenge meant the team were constantly in transit. They slept, ate and relaxed on a tour bus which was a constant hive of activity, with riders nervously preparing for their next episode and riders returning from a hard effort kcen to chat about their experience. Amid this constant commotion they were trying to relax and sleep – a task that proved more difficult for some than others.

Behind the scenes and off camera I worked hard with individual members of the team to ensure they were coping with the rigours of the challenge, taking a different approach with each of them, focusing on their motivations and needs. As a result I spent over 600 miles on the road (sharing the 1,000-mile journey with

Leading lights. The Million Pound Cycle team travelled a thousand miles non-stop from John O'Groats to Land's End supported by a team of outstanding leaders.

my lifelong friend Richard Ball) and managed less than ten hours' sleep across the entire challenge. The ability to lead from the front and remain motivational and inspirational even during your own personal 'dark times' was my own personal triumph as a leader.

After 77 hours of non-stop effort through snow, rain and sun and across the toughest terrain in the UK, the team arrived at Land's End to a heroes' welcome, raising £1.4 million for Sport Relief.

▲ *www.achievetheimpossible.co.uk*

> **TASK**
> - Write your 30-second 'elevator pitch' of your vision statement.
> - Design a reflection grid for your short-, medium- and long-term goals.
> - Design your Leadership Engine and identify dates, times and places for your multi-disciplinary team meetings.

CHAPTER EIGHT

THE DELIVERY OF SUCCESS

Prepare for the worst and hope for the best

It is not uncommon to invest a significant amount of time and effort in creating your vision, planning and preparing for your challenge, and establishing your team only to fall at the final, crucial barrier on your journey along the *road to success*: the delivery. Failure to deliver success can occur at any point along your journey from the start of the challenge to the final steps leading to the finish line.

Early failure and the reasons for yet another 'I was going to, but . . .' challenge are often associated with an overwhelming 'fear of failure', or a 'fear of success' combined with a diminishing 'need to achieve'. This combination of events results in a catastrophic loss of your *brain of success* which can lead to you giving up on a challenge before you have even started.

It is crucial that you address any fears you have and create strategies to overcome them, or accept them and put them to one side, if you are to deliver success. Having addressed your fears, you must create an individually tailored plan for you and your team. Your plan should address every determinant of success and include a detailed series of 'If–Then' scenarios to tackle all possible barriers to success. Ensuring you take rapid and decisive action in the delivery of your 'If–Then' plan and on any unforeseen potholes along your journey will ensure you maintain your speed on your *road to success* and your long-term goal. By never giving up and maintaining your focus on delivering your short-term goals you will deliver success.

By the end of this chapter you will have gained an understanding of:
- An individualized plan of delivery
- The importance of maintaining your *brain of success* through

the planning and preparation phase
- How to pace yourself in the delivery of your long-term goal
- The 2009 Comic Relief 'Red Nose Climb' (challenge highlight)
- How to prepare for the barriers and potholes along your *road to success*
  - Taking rapid and decisive action to reduce the risk of failure
- The 2014 Sport Relief 'Beyond Breaking Point' challenge (challenge highlight)
- How to combat the fear of success and fear of failure by
  - Writing
  - Visualizing
  - Talking
- The importance of never giving up
- Why you should never assume success
- The 2012 Sport Relief 'Walliams versus The Thames' challenge (challenge highlight)
- Tricks of the trade

BESPOKE TAILORING

Every step along the way to delivering your vision requires an individualized approach. From the planning and preparation phase through to establishing your *team of success*, you should be focused on creating an environment which provides an approach specifically tailored to your needs. This remains true for the *delivery of success*. Though the delivery phase is the final stage on your *road to success* you must maintain your focus on providing individualized support for each member of the team. Remember, the team is only as good as each individual member. Making sure you optimize the performance of each team member during delivery will ultimately lead to success.

DON'T LEAVE IT ALL IN TRAINING

In sport it is not uncommon to see athletes who work incredibly hard and produce fantastic performances in training but fail to deliver to the best of their abilities in competition. While commitment to the planning and preparation phase of any challenge is critical, you must avoid ignoring the most important step of delivering success.

The planning and preparation of a challenge can be an incredibly tiring process for you and your team. Developing your long-term goal and creating an environment where you can deliver success places a significant burden on your *brain of success* and those of your team. Maintaining belief, commitment and motivation requires consistent effort that can sometimes be all-encompassing. It is easy to lose sight of your vision and instead expend too much physical and mental energy on getting to the start line. You should constantly check your *brain of success* and ensure the continual top-up of the motivation fuel tank. Well-planned short-term goals act as the service stations along your *road to success*, which provide the critical refuelling required to optimize the belief, commitment and motivation for your challenge. The aim is for you and your team to be in the best possible physical and psychological shape at the start line of your challenge to optimize the *delivery of success*.

PACE YOURSELF

Achieving your short- and medium-term goals is important in maintaining your journey along the *road to success*; however, crossing the finish line and delivering your vision is the ultimate mark of success. Your entire delivery strategy should be planned around the delivery of your long-term goal with your short- and medium-term goals playing a supporting role.

Each goal should be linked to a timeline which provides a

pre-determined time for delivery. Pacing yourself along the *road to success* is important to ensure you continue to deliver your short- and medium-term goals in line with your plan. It is not uncommon to race to deliver your first short-term goals, fuelled by an overflowing motivation fuel tank. Sticking to the plan and controlling your pace of delivery is important if you are to manage your personal resources (energy, belief, commitment, motivation, etc.) appropriately and maintain your speed along your *road to success*.

Delivering your first short-term goals too rapidly usually requires drastic measures and the cutting of corners. This approach is rarely sustainable and often leads to the development of barriers and potholes which slow subsequent progress. For example, if your challenge is weight management, it is relatively easy to hit short-term weight-loss goals ahead of schedule by dramatically decreasing your calorie intake and increasing your physical activity. Unfortunately, this approach often leads to injury and illness and an unsustainable shift in your energy balance. The net result is often failure to deliver your long-term goal. Whether it is a major physical challenge, a personal health challenge or a business challenge, make sure you pace yourself by sticking to your plan. Rapid early gains do not always deliver long-term success.

Challenge Highlight

In 2009, I led the preparation of nine celebrities for a summit attempt of Mount Kilimanjaro for Comic Relief: singer-songwriter Gary Barlow, singers Cheryl Cole, Alesha Dixon, Kimberley Walsh and Ronan Keating, TV presenter Ben Shephard, actress and TV presenter Denise Van Outen and radio and TV presenters Fearne Cotton and Chris Moyles.

The physical and psychological demands of climbing Mt Kilimanjaro present themselves in three ways: the altitude, the climb and the environment. Each of these elements created very different challenges for individual members of the group. The diverse nature of the group meant that an individually tailored solution was required to overcome the barriers to success.

For some, the altitude was a major challenge. The physiological response to altitude is highly variable and difficult to predict. As part of the preparation phase for this challenge I took the group into the environmental chamber at the Centre for Health and Human Performance on London's Harley Street, which was set to replicate 5,000m altitude. It was instantly obvious that certain members of the group were significantly affected while others were not. Ronan Keating suffered badly, for example, having to leave shortly after entry, while Chris Moyles was almost entirely unaffected. This led to the development of individualized altitude plans which included rehydration and nutritional strategies and the use of drugs to reduce the impact of acute mountain sickness (AMS), common on climbs over 3,000m. The use of mild analgesics (paracetamol) and anti-inflammatories (ibuprofen) were supported by a drug called Diamox (acetazolamide – the medication of choice in dealing with AMS) to alleviate symptoms and optimize the *delivery of success*.

The major challenge for Chris Moyles was to be the climb itself: twenty-seven miles uphill over seven days. This may seem a relatively small distance to walk, but for Chris it proved a major challenge which required an individualized approach. Accordingly, during preparation I took Chris and the Radio 1 team up Mount Snowdon – a formidable challenge in the winter snow, ice and sub-zero temperatures. This short-term goal served to support Chris's belief that he could summit Kilimanjaro and also provided an opportunity to develop an individualized pacing strategy which he employed on Mt Kilimanjaro to ensure success.

The final element of environment on Mt Kilimanjaro was also a significant barrier to success for many of the group. For the female contingent, the absence of toilets required a mind-shift in the acceptability of open-air conveniences, while the absence of running water and sleeping in a tent pitched on sloping volcanic rocks would challenge those in the team less experienced at giving up home comforts. For the highly variable challenges faced by each member of the group, the development of an individually tailored delivery strategy was fundamental to ensuring the *delivery of success*.

Arriving at different times on the summit, based on the individually tailored approach, all members of the group successfully summited Mt Kilimanjaro and in doing so helped raise a staggering £3.6 million for Comic Relief.

www.achievetheimpossible.co.uk

Comic Relief Red Nose Climb 2009. Gary Barlow, Chris Moyles and me, along with team members at the summit of Mount Kilimanjaro.

PREPARE FOR THE WORST AND HOPE FOR THE BEST

We have already discussed the need for meticulous planning, including the identification of potential barriers to success and the subsequent production of 'If–Then' scenarios. This process is fundamental during the *delivery of success*. By analysing every determinant of success and identifying all possible barriers you can limit the potential potholes along your *road to success*. This should not be viewed as a negative process but a positive affirmation of your control over the *delivery of success*. Of course, rarely does a journey go smoothly and entirely to plan, therefore you should not view your plan as an immovable object. While you have established your 'If–Then' scenarios for every foreseeable barrier, you must be flexible in your approach during delivery. Be prepared to change your plans to respond rapidly and decisively to potholes. This ability to adapt will limit the potential damage and avoid 'dark times' that can jeopardize the delivery of your long-term goal. By preparing for the worst-case scenarios, you can confidently sit back and hope for the best.

THERE IS NO TIME LIKE THE PRESENT

With a meticulously planned 'If–Then' strategy, you should have solutions to the vast majority of barriers you may face along your journey. However, having solutions is not enough if you are to limit the damage caused by these barriers. The key to maintaining your speed along the *road to success* is to face your problems early and deal with them immediately.

One of the commonest reasons for the premature end to a challenge is the unwillingness to stop and deal with a problem as soon as it arises. Continuing in the face of a problem, hoping that it will miraculously improve without intervention, is a surefire way to end a challenge. What starts off as a barrier with an established solution soon becomes a pothole which can rapidly become a 'dark time'. In my experience it is often the most innocuous of barriers that lead to failure. For example, a blister during an ultra-endurance event which is easily treatable but is ignored for fear of losing momentum soon becomes an open wound which requires significantly more time and is much more difficult to treat. But time is not the enemy in this scenario; of greater concern is the potential for the open wound to become infected, and as a result the challenge is brought to a premature end.

These seemingly minor barriers crop up in all challenges. If your goal is to lose weight or give up smoking it is often the 'just one' excuse that leads to failure. 'Just one cigarette while I'm having a drink' or 'Just one doughnut as a treat' are catastrophic phrases for the *delivery of success*. As you reach barriers along your *road to success* you should act immediately by deploying your solutions. Overcoming barriers not only reduces the negative impact on your journey but can provide positive reaffirmation of your ability to deliver success, leading to greater belief, commitment and motivation, optimizing your *brain of success*.

▲▲ *Challenge Highlight*

Only four hours into her seven-day-long 'Beyond Breaking Point' challenge, Davina McCall hit her first major barrier to success. Having set out in light rain on the 130-mile cycle ride from Edinburgh to the Lake District, we were hit by some of the worst weather I have ever experienced on a bike. A non-stop barrage of torrential snow, sleet, hail and rain was accompanied by winds gusting up to 60mph. Despite months of meticulous planning and preparation, the delivery of this monumental challenge was placed in jeopardy as Davina's *brain of success* started to fail. She began to develop an overwhelming fear of failure which was leading to a very rapid loss in her belief that she could deliver success.

In multi-day ultra-endurance challenges it is not uncommon to be overwhelmed by the enormity of the challenge, particularly in the very early stages. For this reason I always break down the medium-term goal of completing each day into short-term goals linked to 'pit stops'. For day 1 of Davina's challenge, these pit stops were set at *circa* thirty-mile intervals, the purpose of which was to recognize and celebrate successful completion of the short-term goal and create an opportunity to address and resolve any barriers to success.

On this occasion the pit-stop strategy would not do. I had to act fast with the team to ensure that this pothole did not become a 'dark time' and seriously impact on the *delivery of success*. Rather than leave Davina on her bike to battle the fear of failure, I signalled to the team to stop, midway between pit stops, at the side of the road. This unscheduled stop gave me and the team the opportunity to speak to Davina, who was in tears and at what turned out to be one of the lowest points for her on the entire challenge. The brief

Davina McCall's 'Beyond Breaking Point' challenge for Sport Relief 2014 – four hours into day 1. One of the darkest times on her monumental challenge was overcome by rapid and decisive action.

stop allowed me time to reaffirm her belief in her ability to deliver success. I spoke with her about the motivation for her challenge and allowed her to re-establish her total commitment to the challenge.

Reducing her fear of failure and increasing her need to achieve, Davina remounted her bike in weather conditions a professional cyclist would question and continued her journey to success. Seventeen hours after leaving Edinburgh and through the toughest combination of weather and terrain the UK has to offer, Davina reached her first medium-term goal and completed day 1. Only six days to go!

www.achievetheimpossible.co.uk

FEAR OF SUCCESS

Having addressed your *scales of success* and established an environment where the need to achieve outweighs the fear of failure, you must be careful to avoid developing a fear of success. While this may seem like an illogical and unlikely event, it is more common than you might think.

A fear of success is similar to a fear of failure, with many of the same symptoms. It can manifest itself in a variety of ways, ranging from a feeling you somehow don't deserve to be successful, to being afraid of success because it will mean others expect you to continue being successful. The latter is a common reason for being scared of success. For example, those aiming to lose weight are afraid of reaching their goal because they believe their family and friends will expect them to lose even more weight. In major sporting challenges, people often fear successful delivery of short- and medium-term goals as it may increase expectations that they will deliver success in their long-term goal.

The fear of success often leads to self-sabotage, where you begin to procrastinate about the delivery of your goal, unable to make any decisions. This loss of focus is often supported by negative self-talk.

Fear of success, much like fear of failure, will result in damage to your *brain of success*. You will begin to doubt your ability to deliver success and you will lose the motivation to continue. It is not unusual for people to give up on a challenge they are more than capable of completing because they fear the consequences. It is important to remain in the present; focus on achieving your next goal and only project positive images on being successful.

TACKLING YOUR FEARS

And now for another little bit of science to help you on your way to reducing your fear of success or fear of failure (it is not always possible to eliminate fear – we are human after all!). Cognitive-behavioural techniques (an academic's way of saying 'techniques to affect the way we think and behave') are commonly used to change the way a person responds to a situation. When it comes to fear of success there are a number of very simple ways to address your fears and turn a negative into a positive. My three techniques of choice are writing, visualizing and talking.

PUT PEN TO PAPER

By answering a set of simple questions you can identify the likely outcomes of success and replace the negative thoughts of what you fear might happen with positive beliefs about success. Try this simple exercise.

Write down detailed answers to the following questions:

- Why is successfully achieving this goal important to me?
- Do I believe I can deliver success in this goal?
- What is the worst that could happen if I achieve this goal?

- How will my friends and family react if I deliver this goal?
- How committed and motivated am I to achieving this goal?
- Do I believe I deserve to deliver success in this goal?
- What emotions and thoughts am I currently having and what actions am I currently doing to limit my success in delivering this goal?

Using your answers, extract all the positive statements that you have written down and write out a list detailing the positive outcomes of delivering success. Keep this list at hand and read it whenever you begin to fear success.

CLOSE YOUR EYES

Another tool to reduce your fears is to visualize success and everything that comes with it. Try this simple exercise:

- Sit down and close your eyes. Imagine you have successfully delivered your goal.
- Now imagine how you feel about your achievement. Focus only on the positive feelings and keep playing them over in your mind until you have eliminated all negative thoughts.
- Now think about how achieving your goal will affect your life – again, think only of the positive effects and keep playing them over until they become the only outcome of success.

As with physical aspects of performance, you have to train your mind by working hard to develop your visualization skills. Furthermore, as we have discussed with fear of failure and the need to achieve, your fear of success will change on a regular basis, so you will need to continue visualizing success throughout the delivery of your challenge.

TALK TO YOURSELF

During the delivery of a major challenge you will regularly find yourself having an internal conversation in your mind. This conversation is all too often a discussion between good and evil. Your good side puts a positive spin on your ability to achieve success, while your evil side represents your fears of both success and failure. If you do not take charge of this discussion in a rational way it rapidly degrades into an argument. Because you will tend to enter these internal discussions in times of difficulty, the winner will almost always be evil, reinforcing your fears and negatively impacting your *brain of success*.

But you can overcome the dominance of evil by changing what you say to yourself. This positive self-talk is incredibly powerful and has the ability to change who you are. When you think negative thoughts about your ability, you should immediately respond with positive thoughts, reinforcing your defences against the negative thoughts trying to enter your mind. Every positive word you use should be carefully selected as it will direct you to a specific destination. Positive self-talk should lead you directly to the delivery of your goals.

You can create phrases to combat your fears which should be brief, to the point and easily memorized. For positive self-talk to be effective you should be specific about what you want to achieve. Reinforce your belief that you can reach your goal, for instance, by saying, 'I will maintain my target pace because I have achieved it in training.' Alternatively, you should base it on a determinant of success that you fear, so: 'Smoking is bad for my health; I do not want a cigarette.'

It may take time to combat evil so you should repeat yourself on a regular basis. Combining self-talk with visualization can be an incredibly powerful weapon to destroy your fears. As with visualization, the strength of positive self-talking increases with repetition.

A repeated bombardment of good will defeat evil and stop it from returning. Try this simple exercise:

- Think about a good versus evil conversation you have had with yourself recently.
- Now construct a short, positive, catchy phrase to counter your negative thoughts.
- Close your eyes and visualize what achieving the phrase would look and feel like.
- Now re-engage in the conversation in your mind but this time talk to yourself using the phrase and remind yourself of how it would look and feel to achieve your goal.

The combination of writing, visualizing and talking techniques will reduce your fears and optimize the function of your *brain of success*. By taking the right approach you can overcome your fears and deliver success.

SQUEEZE IT OUT

Delivering success is not easy and there are certain to be times when you question your capabilities. One of my favourite self-talk phrases – you will often hear me saying it – is 'squeeze it out'.

The background to this specifically targeted saying is based on a life experience we have all had. Imagine all of your personal resources (your energy, belief, commitment, motivation, etc.) are stored in a tube of toothpaste. When you start a challenge you can press anywhere on the tube with little effort to extract as much of your various resources as you require. Throughout the delivery of a goal you continue to use up your precious resources until, as you near the final stages, you begin to run out of toothpaste. At this stage you need to become more focused, concentrating your efforts on where you can be sure of the best rewards; you need to begin squeezing your toothpaste tube with greater effort for less return. Eventually, you begin to think that your toothpaste tube is empty – and herein lies that life lesson. We have all believed our toothpaste tube to be empty but with focused effort we have always managed to squeeze enough out to brush our teeth one more time.

The same is true of our own natural resources: as you start to feel that you can't go on, that there is nothing left to give, just 'squeeze it out' and you will find more is in you. The combination of positive self-talk and visualization in this example is a powerful tool which demonstrates that with a little extra effort and focused application you will be able to deliver those precious resources you need to deliver success.

IT'S ALL IN THE DETAIL

Another reason for the development of a fear of success and a fear of failure is a perceived loss of control over the challenge. As part of your *road to success* you have produced a *wheel of success* identifying the determinants of success. Alongside these determinants you have planned a detailed approach to optimizing each element of performance, and through the Profile-Prescribe-Monitor model you are able to track improvements in performance which are then reflected by changes on your *wheel of success*. This detailed approach may, at times, seem burdensome; but it is of fundamental importance in enhancing your *brain of success* and reducing your fears. In delivering this approach you must recognize your role as leader of your *team of success*. While you are not responsible for delivering all aspects of the challenge, maintaining control of the team and overseeing their work provides you with the knowledge you require to reduce your fears.

It is possible to suffer from fear of success and fear of failure at the same time. In this situation you may feel completely paralysed by indecision while you balance every decision against these fears. By identifying strategies to optimize every element of performance and maintaining control of your challenge, you will reduce your fears, enhance the function of your *brain of success* and optimize the delivery of your vision.

NEVER GIVE UP

Failure is not an option. You must always focus on success and do not allow yourself to entertain thoughts of failure. Think of thoughts of failure like rust on your car: once you allow a spot of rust to develop, it will spread until your whole car is affected. In your mind, failure can take over in the same way and negatively impact on the *delivery of success*. It is important to stop the rust of failure developing by tackling it on a continual basis.

We have discussed the use of techniques to overcome our fears, but one of the major drivers of failure is failure itself. A catastrophic loss of belief, commitment and motivation can lead to your giving up on a goal. By promoting the belief that you cannot deliver success, you are much more likely to fail in the delivery of future goals. Once you have given up on a goal it is much more difficult to return to the same goal and deliver success.

Weight management is a classic example of this, where giving up on a short-term weight-loss goal leads to continued future failure. By not achieving a target weight, fears of being unable to achieve success are reinforced. As a result of strengthening fears, a set of excuses develops to explain future failure, often before it has happened. This leads to a downward spiral of failure, eventually leading to your giving up on the long-term goal completely. This is why you should pay constant attention to your *brain of success* and never give up.

It is important to remember that giving up is not the same as failing to deliver a goal. Meticulous planning and preparation should reduce the potential for failure; however, as we have already discussed, there may be potholes along the *road to success* that impact on your ability to deliver success. These events are only failures if we fail to learn from them. Having revised your plans, transforming the pothole into a barrier and creating an 'If–Then' plan to limit its future impact, you are in a position to recommence your journey. Tackling these potholes in this way provides positive reinforcement of your ability to deliver success.

THE HERE AND NOW

You can often find yourself overwhelmed with the enormity of a major challenge. Focusing on the long-term goal can lead you to question your belief in your ability to deliver success, leading to a reduction in commitment and motivation. In these situations it is important that you refocus your attention on the goal at hand. Concentrating your efforts on delivering a short-term goal will seem much more achievable, giving you the confidence to continue working hard to deliver success. If you look after the short-term goals, the long-term goals look after themselves!

It is not uncommon in the later stages of a major challenge to feel that even the short-term goals may be beyond your capabilities. This is certainly true of major physical challenges when your personal resources (energy, belief, motivation, commitment, etc.) are in the 'red zone'. In these moments you should set yourself immediate short-term goals which you can achieve rapidly, allowing you to maintain your progress to the finish line. For example, towards the end of an ultra-endurance run, an immediate short-term goal would be to count a hundred steps. By repeating this immediate short-term goal over and over again you will constantly achieve success, which reaffirms your belief that you can reach your long-term goal. By adding positive self-talk to this process you can increase the strength of the message you are sending your *brain of success*. For example, 'Every step completed is a step closer to the finish'. Whatever the challenge, it is always important to maintain your focus on the here and now: one day at a time; one hour at a time; one step at a time.

NEVER ASSUME

Major challenges can falter at the final few barriers along the *road to success*. It is easy to lose focus and assume that you have delivered success before you have crossed the finish line. This assumption of success can occur at any point during delivery, from standing on the start line at the very beginning of the challenge to the final few steps before the finish line. Having prepared for the worst, it is sometimes difficult not to become over-confident in your abilities and think the challenge is easier to deliver than it is. This over-confidence can lead to catastrophic damage to your *brain of success* when you realize it is going to be very tough to deliver success.

You should never assume you have delivered success until you have crossed the finish line. It is a mistake to start celebrating before you have achieved your long-term goal. The final steps of a major challenge are as difficult as the initial steps, sometimes harder. You must remain realistic about the challenge you face and manage your expectations and those of your team to ensure you maintain focus. Keep focused on delivering your goal until you have crossed the finish line and the fat lady has started singing!

Challenge Highlight

In September 2011, comedian, actor and writer David Walliams began a challenge to swim 140 miles along the Thames for Sport

Relief. Only five years after successfully swimming the Channel, the 'blue riband' of open-water swims, David would need to swim a similar distance every day for eight consecutive days.

'Walliams versus The Thames' was without doubt one of the toughest challenges I have led. One of the key issues that arose for this challenge was 'assumption' on a number of levels. Firstly, it was the twelfth challenge I had led for Comic/Sport Relief and with eleven successful challenges delivered there was an air of assumption that this would be another ticked box. Secondly, David had successfully swum the Channel and the Strait of Gibraltar, and captained The Million Pound Cycle; with this pedigree the Thames would simply be another in a long line of outstanding achievements. Thirdly, the team that worked on this challenge, including the logistics team Threshold Sports, the Comic Relief team and the BBC documentary team, had been part of the successful delivery of a number of challenges, which also fuelled the assumption of success.

It was, however, short-lived. For the first three-hour section (the first short-term goal) David chose to swim without a wetsuit. Following an unseasonably cold summer the water temperature was a very chilly 11°C. By the end of the three hours it became apparent that David was suffering from hypothermia, evidenced by a combination of physical appearance (a blue hue to his upper back and splaying of fingers) and confusion and slurred speech.

On exiting the water, I worked hard with the team to warm David up – not a simple task as body temperature drops rapidly on exit from cold water due to a process known as the 'after-drop', and the fact that you must not re-warm too quickly for fear of complications. Hypothermia poses a real danger to life as well as leading to the potential failure of the challenge. Fortunately, David Walliams is one of the toughest people I have ever met and his drive and determination to continue meant that just thirty minutes after stopping we entered the water together for the next three-hour stage, this time both wearing wetsuits to reduce the ongoing impact of the cold.

David Walliams's challenge for Sport Relief 2012, 'Walliams versus The Thames'. The return to swimming following the team's realization of the enormity of the challenge that lay ahead.

Confidence is central to the success of any challenge, and to that end an assumption of success can be a very valuable commodity if it is supported by meticulous planning, preparation and delivery. The expertise and experience of a truly outstanding team combined with the truly outstanding *brain of success* possessed by David Walliams led to the successful completion of this iconic challenge on the steps of Westminster Bridge, 140 miles and eight days after leaving the start of the navigable Thames in Lechlade.

www.achievetheimpossible.co.uk

TRICKS OF THE TRADE

Experience is a valuable commodity when taking on a major challenge. Having undertaken a major challenge before provides you with knowledge that can at the very least support you on your journey along the *'road to success'* and can sometimes be the difference between success and failure. That said, you do not require experience to deliver success. The steps detailed in this book provide the road map which, if followed carefully, will optimize your *delivery of success*. In addition to this meticulously structured approach, you should always tap into your experience of previous challenges or the experience of others as these can provide you with additional information that may reduce the number of barriers and potholes to success. Some of the most valuable experiences are those that create solutions to some of the unusual problems, particularly those associated with reducing the pain and therefore increasing the enjoyment of the journey. Throughout your journey you will develop your own solutions to unforeseen problems (potholes), but careful investigation of your own and others' experiences may have already provided you with a solution which can then be integrated into an 'If–Then' plan for that barrier. Here are some examples of unusual solutions I have developed during major challenges.

'FANNY FUDGE'

During Davina McCall's 'Beyond Breaking Point' challenge one of the major issues she faced was abrasions around her groin as a result of wearing wet cycling shorts over a prolonged period of time (up to seventeen hours per day). The challenge doctor (Dr Matthew Stride), physiotherapist (Mark Perkins) and I developed a cream which was a combination of a barrier cream (commonly used for nappy rash) and a local anaesthetic cream. This cream instantly solved Davina's problem and increased her enjoyment dramatically.

Cycling in the rain. Responding to the problem immediately and creating a unique solution kept Davina on her bike and on course for success.

COLD AND TIGHT

During John Bishop's 'Week of Hell' challenge, one of the major issues he faced was muscle damage, which results in significant pain and a reduction in performance. Muscle damage is not unusual in sport. It's a problem that has been researched and a number of solutions have been developed. I have used these solutions across the sport and exercise spectrum to reduce muscle damage in both elite athletes and first-time challengers. For John Bishop, the remedy was ice baths for his legs at the completion of every day. Cooling the legs in 10°C water for ten minutes reduces inflammation and subsequent damage. Ice baths can be a miserable experience but the short-term pain leads to long-term gain. Immediately following the ice bath John would wear compression tights which further reduced damage during sleep. Finally, John consumed a special antioxidant supplement and a protein shake to assist in muscle repair. This

In deep water. Using evidence-based interventions to reduce the impact of muscle damage allowed John Bishop to continue his 'Week of Hell'.

combination of factors, which has been developed through experience, resulted in reduced muscle damage, less pain and enhanced performance.

STRAPPED UP

In addition to muscle damage, one of the key issues for Eddie Izzard during his forty-three marathons in fifty-one days was abrasion damage to the feet leading to painful blisters and open wounds. There were a number of developments which I used to reduce the damage. Firstly, experience has taught me that wearing shoes half a size larger than normal and changing the shoes on a rotating basis each day can significantly reduce abrasions. The use of a sock liner (ultra-thin with no seams) or double-lined socks, which I developed from previous challenges, further reduces the potential for abrasion. Finally, the use of specialist tape and an aggressive approach

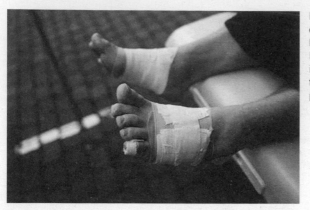

In good shape. Despite the completion of forty-two of his forty-three marathons Eddie Izzard's feet are still in remarkable condition due to the individualized and proactive treatment plan.

to blisters and abrasions significantly prevents the worsening of problems. With this package of interventions to reduce muscle and feet damage Eddie was able to complete his forty-three marathons intact.

GREASED UP

Two major issues for David Walliams during his 'Walliams versus The Thames' challenge were the cold and wetsuit abrasions. The cold is a major problem for both health and performance, and given the 11°C water temperatures for up to fourteen hours a day it was a barrier for which I had to provide a solution. The answer was to use a thermal vest, which I had previously used to combat cold immersion in a previous challenge. The thermal vest is worn under the wetsuit and increases skin temperature by around 2°C – enough to block the insidious misery of the cold. For the skin abrasions, which were significant, we had to develop a new answer, which came in the form of a combination of pre-existing products. A synthetic skin covered by a mixture of barrier cream and petroleum jelly which remained in place despite the hours of constant immersion and abrasion was the solution. The combined effect of warming and pain reduction reduced the misery and enhanced performance.

The pain of success. David prepares for another gruelling fourteen hours of swimming supported by bespoke interventions to reduce the impact of the cold and open sores.

By using your own experience or the experience of others to identify and implement solutions you can avoid 'dark times' and potholes and limit the impact of barriers. Major challenges are what they say on the tin: they are a challenge. Smoothing your road to success by using these 'tricks of the trade' does not reduce the scale of the challenge but can improve your experience in the *delivery of success*. By reducing the misery you will enhance your experience, leading to greater satisfaction, which will provide you with the platform to take on further challenges in the future. Your aim is to reach your destination and successfully deliver your long-term goal by the shortest and smoothest route possible. In general, short-cuts do not exist; however, experience can reduce the possibility of your taking a wrong turn, resulting in a longer route than is absolutely necessary.

TASK
- Together with your team, write down your detailed plan for the delivery of your vision.
  - Ensure it is individualized for you and every member of your *team of success*.
- Construct an 'If–Then' plan to deal with every barrier to success.
  - Leave nothing to chance; carefully scrutinize every determinant of success.
- Identify any goals that create a fear of success.
- For each of these goals, take your time in writing down detailed answers to the following questions:
  - Why is successfully achieving this goal important to me?
  - Do I believe I can deliver success in this goal?
  - What is the worst that could happen if I achieve this goal?
  - How will my friends and family react if I deliver this goal?
  - How committed and motivated am I to achieving this goal?
  - Do I believe I deserve to deliver success in this goal?
  - What thoughts am I currently having and what actions am I currently doing to limit my success in delivering this goal?
- Visualize yourself achieving success.
- Construct a short, positive, memorable phrase to counter your negative thoughts for each of your fears.
- Practise combining visualization and self-talk until you have overcome all your fears.

CHAPTER NINE

THE PERFECT STORM FOR SUCCESS

Turning the impossible into an achievement

The *road to success* is strewn with barriers, potholes and 'dark times' which have, at best, the potential to slow your journey or, at worst, bring a premature end to your challenge. Having overcome the first and often highest barrier to success, vision, you should identify the short- and medium-term goals which act as critical signposts along your *road to success*. While delivering success in each individual short-term goal is relatively straightforward to achieve, the key to success is the repeated delivery of all short- and medium-term goals, leading to your long-term goal.

The mark of excellence is not the ability to deliver a one-off success, it is the ability to replicate success throughout your entire journey. Such sustained success is not a chance event. Understanding your long-term goal and the determinants of success will enable you to identify your strengths and weaknesses. Profiling yourself against each of the determinants, prescribing individually tailored interventions and monitoring your progress will optimize the movement of each of your determinants to the outer ring of excellence on your *wheel of success*.

None of this can be achieved alone. You must appoint a *team of success* to support you along your journey. The appointment of a team is not in itself enough to ensure success. For your team to reach its full potential and have the greatest positive impact on your performance you must fully integrate each member of the team and manage them to optimize their performance.

With your vision and *team of success* in place you should meticulously plan and prepare your journey along the *road to success*. Individual tailoring of macro-, meso- and micro-cycles around your goals provides the foundations upon which your *road to success* is built. Throughout your journey you will need to pay close attention to your *brain of success* to ensure you maintain your belief, commitment and motivation in delivering your vision. Finally, the *delivery of success* requires a maintained focus on your long-term goal, continued effort and meticulous planning. Bringing it all together will create the *perfect storm for success* and optimize the delivery of your vision, making the impossible, possible.

By the end of this chapter you will have gained an understanding of:
- The complexity of the limits to success
- The steps required to deliver the *perfect storm for success*
- The role of self-reflection
- The importance of celebrating success
- Setting a new challenge following success
- The value of enjoyable times during your challenge
- Challenge highlights

THE MODEL OF SUCCESS

The limits to success are based on a large number of factors within four areas: Body, Mind, Technical and Environment. Performance is therefore made up of a complex bio-psycho-social interaction of factors which must be understood and addressed if success is to be delivered. By constructing a Model of Success you can examine the factors that limit performance, which provides you with an overview of the key areas of focus. By addressing each of the limiting factors you will enhance your ability to reduce the impact of all limits to performance and in doing so optimize your *delivery of success*.

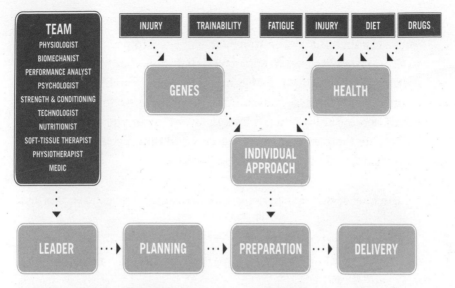

The Model of Success – the complex bio-psycho-social model of human athletic performance. Note the central importance of the leader (coach) who is responsible for appointing, integrating and leading the large team of specialists, and the individualized planning and preparation taking into account all determinants of success together with barriers to success. The entire model is surrounded by the sociological environment which impacts every aspect of performance.

THE JOURNEY TO SUCCESS

The delivery of your long-term goal will not happen simply because you want it to. You must take a structured, systematic approach if you are to optimize the *delivery of success*. The Journey to Success is simple in structure but requires a pragmatic approach in its delivery. There are no short-cuts on the *road to success*; you must deliver each step in order. Bypassing any of the steps will at best slow your progress and at worst lead to failure. Furthermore, you should aim to deliver excellence at each step. Success breeds success: if you and your team focus on optimizing performance at each step, you will progressively build towards the delivery of your long-term goal.

The Journey to Success.
Using a structured approach you will create the *perfect storm for success* and optimize the delivery of your vision.

Despite the structural simplicity of the Journey to Success, the *delivery of success* is more complex. Each step along your *road to success* requires a careful, meticulous approach to deliver the essential elements for successful completion of each step and the ultimate delivery of your long-term goal. Optimizing your *brain of success* throughout this process is critical if you are to maintain your progress along your *road to success* and deliver your long-term goal. Careful attention should be paid to addressing the function of your *brain of success* throughout your journey. By following the steps detailed in this book and outlined below you will create your *perfect storm for success.*

THE *VISION OF SUCCESS*

Establishing your vision is the first step along your *road to success*. Ensuring the challenge is important to you and that you fully understand the time and resource requirements of the challenge provide the foundation on which to build your road map. Having established your vision you should clearly define the goals along your *road to success*. Complete the following two steps:

- Answer the questions of destiny and write down your vision
- Set your short-, medium- and long-term SMART goals by passing them through the goal flow

THE DETERMINANTS OF SUCCESS

Identifying the component parts of success and profiling yourself against the 'gold standard' allows you to develop an understanding of your strengths and weaknesses. This initial profile provides you with the information required to design an individually tailored prescription that you should monitor on a regular basis. In addition to identifying the determinants of success you should identify all barriers to success and create solutions for each barrier. Complete the following three steps:

- Construct your *wheel of success*
- Establish a balance in favour of your need to achieve
- Identify barriers to success and produce your 'If–Then' tables

THE *TEAM OF SUCCESS*

Delivering success is never a lone quest. Irrespective of the size of the challenge you will require the best team around you to optimize your *delivery of success*. Ensuring you surround yourself with specialists who can provide the knowledge, skills and experience required to support the delivery of your long-term goal is a critical step along your *road to success*. Complete the following three steps:

- Construct your Team Tyre
- Identify your team members and team leaders
- Appoint, integrate and optimize the performance of your team members

THE *ROAD TO SUCCESS*

Planning and preparation are fundamental to the *delivery of success*. You cannot rely on chance; you must carefully structure your plan to ensure you move each determinant of success to the outer ring of excellence on your *wheel of success*. Using your short-, medium- and long-term goals you should construct micro-, meso- and macrocycles which provide meticulous detail on how you are going to deliver success. Having established your cycles you should then use the principles of preparation to deliver your goals. Complete the following three steps:

- Design your macro-cycle
- Design your meso-cycle
- Construct your first micro-cycle

THE *DELIVERY OF SUCCESS*

Having spent a significant amount of time, effort and resources on your challenge you must not lose focus at the most important stage of your journey: the delivery. You must design and implement a detailed plan of delivery which includes your solutions to overcome all barriers you will face during the final steps along your *road to success*. Complete the following four steps:

- Write down a detailed plan for the *delivery of success*
- Construct 'If–Then' plans for all barriers to success
- Identify any aspects of your challenge that create a fear of failure and fear of success
- Create written, self-talk and visualization strategies to establish a balance in favour of your need to achieve

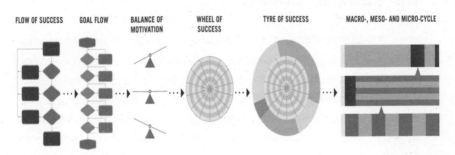

The *perfect storm for success*. Taking a structured, systematic approach and completing each step to the best of your ability will optimize your *delivery of success*.

A CELEBRATION OF SUCCESS

Achieving your long-term goal is the primary aim of your challenge. However, the reason underlying the development of your vision should be directly linked to one outcome: improving the quality of your life and, directly or indirectly, the lives of your family and friends. With this outcome in mind you should ensure that you take the time at the end of a major challenge to enjoy the fruits of your labour and thank those who have been instrumental in the delivery of your success.

During your planning you identified the reward for delivering your long-term goal. Having delivered on your vision you should ensure that you follow through with the reward and give yourself time to enjoy and reflect upon your achievement. Rewarding yourself will reinforce the positive impact on your life of achieving your long-term goal. By making the award public you can further reinforce the positive impact by gaining external recognition. A public statement of success also gives you the opportunity to recognize and be grateful for the contribution of your team. This process is important for your team's *brain of success* and provides a platform from which to build future major challenges with the same *team of success*.

A word of caution: it is critical that you fully appreciate your success and be entirely satisfied with the delivery of your long-term goal. It is a common mistake to move on too quickly to the next challenge without allowing yourself time to absorb your success. This lack of fulfilment often leads to an unhealthy obsession to achieve, devoid of any appreciation of success. This approach can be damaging for your own quality of life and can negatively impact on those close to you. Take the time to recognize your success and appreciate what you and your team have achieved.

REFLECTING ON SUCCESS

We have already spoken about the need for reflection on reaching your goals using your rear-view mirror of success (see Chapter 7 – The Leadership of Success). Reflecting on the delivery of short- and medium-term goals leads to improvements which smooth your journey along the *road to success*. The completion of your challenge should not signify the end of this reflective practice. Reflecting on the successful delivery of your long-term goal is an important process that builds your experience, which is invaluable for future challenges.

It can be more important to analyse success compared with failure, yet it is not uncommon to spend excessive amounts of time deliberating over failure while success is instantly accepted as an expected outcome. Once you have celebrated your success, take time to write down the aspects of the challenge that were successful and unsuccessful. Bringing together all of the experiences you have gathered from your reflective practice throughout your challenge will provide invaluable information for future challenges. This process should be undertaken in three stages:

- Using your 'If–Then' tables, write down those solutions that worked to overcome the barriers along your *road to success*.
- Write down the solutions created to address potholes on your journey.
- Write a detailed account of the causes of any 'dark times' and how you overcame them to continue your journey.

Combining your reflections on each of these areas will furnish you with a template for your 'If–Then' tables on future challenges, providing solutions for the barriers to success and reducing the potential for potholes and 'dark times'.

If (risk to performance)	Then (solution to the risk)	Outcome	Adaptations to 'If–Then'
If I get a puncture on the road when I am alone	Then I will change the inner tube and inform the team at the next stop that I have used my spare tube and gas refill	The plan was successful until I punctured for a second time and had no gas	Carry two gas refills and consider carrying a pump

If my chain breaks	**Then** I will call my support team to let them know my chain has broken and that I am attempting to fix it myself. I will ask the team to start heading towards my location and I will call them once I have fixed the chain	Chain did not break	Continue to use same 'If–Then' strategy
If my lights are running low on battery	**Then** I will use my spare light which I am carrying with me and inform the team at the next stop	The system worked well until we forgot to charge the spare light	Put a plan in place to plug all battery-powered devices in at the end of every night section
If my wheel is buckled	**Then** I will call my support team to meet me at my location to change the wheel	Wheels did not buckle	Continue to use same 'If–Then' strategy
If my gears are not changing smoothly or are jumping	**Then** I will inform my support team at the next stop and have them repaired	The 'If–Then' plan was effectively deployed on several occasions	Add a mechanical service of the bike every day to reduce tuning issues
If I have a catastrophic failure of my bike	**Then** I will call my support team to tell them what has happened and where to meet me. I will then put my jacket on and find shelter until the team arrive.	No catastrophic failure	Continue to use same 'If–Then' strategy

Reflecting on the 'If–Then' plan following the successful delivery of the long-term goal.
Note: the adapted 'If–Then' plan becomes the new 'If–Then' plan for the next challenge.

THE FUN TIMES

Enjoyment is the essence of a successful challenge. Major challenges require a huge amount of time, effort and sacrifice; but it is rare for us to remember the misery. The default position for many of us is to look at challenges through rose-tinted spectacles and remember only the enjoyable moments of a major challenge. The capacity to store positive memories and forget the misery is an evolutionary quality that provides us with the ability to continue in the face of adversity.

It is often said that pain is short-lived but success lasts a lifetime. When it comes to memories of the *road to success*, your ability to recall the enjoyable moments of the journey is important in reflecting on success and providing the platform from which to start your next challenge. To that end, it is important that you build

Happy days! Me and David Walliams after a long swim in the tidal Thames laughing about our first experience of swimming through treated sewage.

215

enjoyable moments into your challenge and remember to value the unplanned fun times along the way too.

A CHANGE IS AS GOOD AS A REST

Successful delivery of your vision does not have to be the end but should mark the beginning of a new journey. It is not uncommon to feel a sense of depression or emptiness following the delivery of a long-term goal. The time and effort required to deliver success often means that major challenges can take over your life and provide the stimulus to your *brain of success*, not only for the challenge but for life in general. Once the challenge is complete you may find your *brain of success* is down-regulated for family, friends and/or work. You must take proactive action to combat this common problem.

Accordingly, having celebrated your success and reflected on your achievement, you will find that setting a new long-term goal can be incredibly rewarding and reinforce the positive changes you have made to your life. The new challenge does not have to be an extension of your previous challenge. While you have developed belief in your ability to deliver success, your *brain of success* may falter in delivering the same, albeit modified, long-term goal. This is invariably due to a diminished motivation, leading to a loss of commitment. Repeating success in the same goal is incredibly challenging and requires a huge effort to maintain motivation and commitment. This is a problem faced by elite athletes on a continual basis as they strive to make tiny improvements to the same performance throughout their careers.

That said, you can build upon your previous success by choosing a different goal that helps support the achievement of your last long-term goal. For example, if you successfully achieved your long-term goal of weight loss, rather than setting yourself a new target weight, why not try an exercise challenge like running a 5km? The challenge of this different long-term goal will optimize your *brain of success* and the training required to complete your challenge will keep you physically active and help you make better diet and lifestyle choices, which support your ability to maintain your weight loss in the long term.

CHANGING LIVES

Taking on a major challenge and delivering success will change your life for the better. The knowledge, skills and experience that you gain during the planning, preparation and delivery of your challenge will be transferable to other areas of your life. The development of your communication skills in selecting and integrating your team and optimizing their performance is a valuable asset that will enhance your personal and work life.

Alongside the knowledge, skills and experience you develop during your challenge, delivering success will change how you view yourself and how others view you. Successfully delivering your goals provides palpable evidence upon which confidence is built. You will develop an 'I can' attitude to life, a belief that you can deliver success in other areas of life, giving you the confidence to take on new challenges.

In addition to how you view yourself, others will view you differently. This change can be profound, leading to your family, friends and colleagues (even people you don't know) treating you differently, in a more positive light. Delivering success in a major challenge does not solely result in a short-term benefit. The impact of success can last long into the future and with the setting of new challenges you will not only change your life for the better, you will change your life for ever.

The best example of the life-changing power of major challenges I have been part of was the *This Morning* Channel swim.

Each member of the team experienced a life-enhancing response to achieving their long-term goal of swimming the Channel, but it was for one of the team in particular that life changed dramatically. Mel's breast cancer had resulted, as it often does in cancer sufferers, in a dramatic change in her own and in others' belief in what she was able to achieve. The seemingly impossible challenge of swimming the Channel was often regarded as a step too far. But on 2 August 2007, the impossible became possible, and with that Mel erased the view of herself as a 'cancer sufferer' and replaced it with the title 'Channel swimmer'. The impact of achieving that success changed her life and those close to her; even beyond that, it is a story of hope and inspiration that has changed the lives of many.

CHALLENGE HIGHLIGHTS

In addition to the *delivery of success* in numerous personal major challenges, I have worked with clients to deliver success across the entire spectrum of performance, from cancer patients facing major surgery to weight management in morbidly obese individuals, and from elite athletes aiming for Olympic glory to businessmen attempting to summit Everest.

Among this group the highest profile and at times the most difficult have been the eighteen Comic Relief and Sport Relief challenges I have supported since 2006. Achieving success in each of these major challenges required the same systematic approach to ensure success: establishing the vision; appointing, integrating and optimizing performance of a *team of success*; planning and preparation along the *road to success*; and delivering success.

While these component parts of the overall strategy for success remained the same, the size and complexity of each Comic Relief and Sport Relief challenge, together with the wide-ranging knowledge, skills and experience of the celebrities and team, led to unique barriers, potholes and 'dark times'. Developing an individually tailored approach to your challenge is crucial in optimizing the *delivery of success*.

Surrounding every major challenge is the belief by some that success is impossible to achieve. This has been true for all the major challenges I have led, including the Comic Relief and Sport Relief challenges. 'Impossible' is an overused word, too often employed by those who lack vision, who use it as an excuse to avoid major challenges in life. You should be careful not to allow this ever-present background noise to impact on your belief in your ability to deliver success.

In contrast, the negativity of a few can act as a potent positive support for your *brain of success*, as long as you have clearly established a balance between your need to achieve and fear of failure and success. Proving people wrong and achieving your goals can be one of the greatest rewards for success, but make sure you and your team consistently maintain belief, commitment and motivation.

To optimize your *brain of success* you should focus on surrounding yourself with those who share your belief, commitment and motivation. The essence of success throughout the Comic Relief and Sport Relief challenges has been the positivity which surrounds the celebrities on a continuous basis. From the very first Sport Relief challenge, David Walliams's 'Big Swim', to the most recent, Davina McCall's 'Beyond Breaking Point', there has been a sustained low-level background noise of 'impossibility'. But while these challenges have consistently pushed the celebrities to the limits of their capabilities, the belief of all those involved in the challenge has resulted in a 100% success rate. This provides evidence of one fact: *nothing* is impossible.

Optimizing the function of your *brain of success* is central to success. The principal motivator for all of the Comic Relief and Sport Relief challenges has been fundraising. To that end, the success of these challenges is not only measured by crossing the finish line; it also lies in the £33 million raised to support the effort of creating a just world, free from poverty.

Irrespective of the size and complexity of your challenge, one overarching truth remains: success is not a chance event. This book has detailed my approach to delivering success, whoever you are or whatever your vision. By adopting the systematic approach outlined in the previous chapters and tailoring it to you and your challenge you will create the *perfect storm for success*, and in doing so optimize the delivery of your vision and achieve the impossible.

Success is not a chance event. Eighteen challenges, £33 million, and the transformation of lives in the UK and around the world – when the impossible became the possible.

ACKNOWLEDGEMENTS

Writing this book has been a major challenge and as such I have practised what I have preached and followed the model I have detailed here. Of all the chapters in the book, Chapter 6 – The Team of Success details the importance of the team in delivering success. To that end, I must thank the following team members for their support, guidance, wisdom and friendship in producing what I hope is a useful guide for all of life's challenges.

Firstly, my thanks go to the team at Transworld Publishers. To my commissioning editor, Giles Elliott, whose enthusiasm for this project has been an inspiration only surpassed by his love of all things sport! To Micaela Alcaino, Phil Lord and Alison Martin for their expertise in the design and production of the book; to Alison Barrow and Ben Willis for their crucial support with publicity; and to key members of the publishing team including: Zoe Willis, Becky Smith, Gary Harley, Suzanne Riley, Polly Osborn, Helen Edwards, Helen Gregory and Yasmin Kidwai.

I must thank the entire team at Comic Relief who are far too numerous to be listed in full. However, particular mentions must go to: Kevin Cahill, legend and CEO; Mark Woods, social-media guru; Stephen Meadows, Kate Adams and Alan Pomroy, project managers extraordinaire; Rick Scott, Vanessa Russo, Rebecca Allan-Cavanaugh, Dean Swift and Mariama Abudulai, the artist-liaison dream team; Karl Reynolds, fundraising master; Chris Wilson, media king; and Lucy McGill, Sophie King and Jess Ord, PR gurus. Thank you for the opportunity and the fabulous times we have spent together.

The team at Threshold Sports whose attention to detail and tireless work ethic have been instrumental in delivering success across so many of the projects detailed in this book. Particular thanks to Julian Mack, Cassie Down, Amanda Dunkley and Amanda Hedley-Lewis.

Thanks to the staff and students at Liverpool John Moores University for supporting my work, and to the discipline of sport and exercise science that has, in part, provided me with the knowledge, skills and experiences to create the model of success detailed in this book. Particular thanks go to Professor Keith George, Professor Tim Cable and Professor Dave Richardson.

To the team at the Centre for Health & Human Performance for their continued support in delivering excellence to all of their clients, many of whom have achieved, and continue to achieve, success in life's biggest challenges.

Thanks to the team at The Sports Sphere for their invaluable guidance and making this book a reality. In particular my agent, James Harper, and PR manager, Milly Baker.

Finally, but most importantly, I want to thank my family. My dad, my hero, who taught me the value of hard work and dedication, and my wife Penny and our three fabulous children, Maya, Elise and Mitchell, for supporting me more than I feel I support them at times!

I hope that I have done them proud and together we have produced a book that will help you deliver success and Achieve the Impossible.

ABOUT THE AUTHOR

Greg Whyte is an internationally recognized expert in the field of physiology, sports and exercise performance.

Professor of Applied Sport and Exercise Science at Liverpool John Moores University and Director of the Centre for Health and Human Performance in London's Harley Street, he has extensive experience of assessing, treating and improving the performance of people ranging from cancer sufferers, celebrities attempting charity challenges to elite athletes.

An Olympian and both European and world championship medallist in modern pentathlon, he was awarded the OBE for his services to Sport, Sports Science and Charity in 2014.

For more information about Professor Greg Whyte, see his website at www.achievetheimpossible.co.uk